le 2ᵉ Decembre

Nick Branly

(courtesy of Alex)

THEATRE LORE

REVISED EDITION
(see Back Cover)

Did you ever catch
my Chekov at Crewe?

LAST NIGHT'S PRODUCTION
PRESENTS

THEATRE LORE

A DICTIONARY
OF
BACKSTAGE LANGUAGE, EXPRESSIONS
AND
USEFUL STAGE KNOWLEDGE

FOR THOSE THEATRICALLY BENT
OR
OF A CURIOUS NATURE

By
NICK BROMLEY

Illustrations By
SIMON BOND

Foreword By
SIMON CALLOW

To Andrea

Published in the United Kingdom in 2012 by
LNP Books
35 Westville Road
London
W12 9BB

This edition published in 2016

ISBN 978-0-9572683-0-2

Cover design and formatting by Duncan Hook

Printed and bound in the UK by 4edge Limited

This book can be ordered direct from the publisher at
http://www.lnpbooks.co.uk

FOREWORD
By Simon Callow

You will not find a definition of the job of Company Stage Manager in these informative and provocative pages. But that is the profession to which the author belongs: one of those fearless men and women who stand at the interface between the management and the show, between the technicians and the creatives, between the actors and the public, between anarchy and order, between tears and laughter.

In other words, Company Stage Managers are, in the theatre, all things to all men and women (and, in the less fortunate cases, children and animals). They devise schedules, they co-ordinate scene changes, they pay actors, they attempt to instil both discipline and harmony into the daily workings of the show, they mediate, Solomon-like, between those who bear grudges against each other, they calm down directors in despair, they hold authors' hands when no one else will speak to them, they go out front, to the public areas, and smell the mood; in a crisis, they take over the calling of the cues and the running of the technical aspect of the show.

On tour, they supervise the getting in and the getting out of the set, they ensure that everyone is accommodated, they find out about the local gyms at which concessions are available, they find out which restaurants are cheap, which are good, and which are guaranteed to give you ptomaine poisoning. In the case of the latter, they call the rehearsals at which the understudy will be put on; indeed, they rehearse the understudies during the day while the rest of the cast is swaggering around town, hoping for compliments on last night's performances.

They arrange visits to laryngologists, physiotherapists, gynaecologists, and psychoanalysts. They act as marriage guidance counsellors; they sit with the star as he nurses a very large scotch whisky and contemplates the decline of his career; they ensure that there is a bottle or two of something decent in the office in case unexpected guests turn up backstage.

They are, in short, gods among men (and women), without whom nothing whatever would happen in the theatre. And the prince among these god-like men is the author of this book. I have rejoiced in his services both as actor and director; I have marvelled that, despite all the many functions he discharges, he has taken note of life as it lurches past him, he has spotted this quirk here and that anomaly there and laughed, he has anticipated this problem and that he has done the necessary to stop it getting out of hand. He is, in fact, like the conductor of a great orchestra: nothing escapes his attention.

That is why you should read this book, and why you should believe what it tells you, however strange it may seem. This is the life of the theatre viewed from the ground floor, from the front line, from the boiler room, from the sidelines, from the touchline.

This is the theatre like it really, really is. Never mind high-falutin' books written by people like the author of this tiny foreword, prating of Art and Anguish: this is the reality, the *traintrain journalier*, as the French (well, some of them) say: the daily grind. It may come as a bit of a surprise...

INTRODUCTION

Bookshop shelves are groaning these days under the weight of countless reference guides and textbooks all about the meaning of drama, the technicalities of working in the theatre and the language of the stage.

They are, I am glad to say, written with the best of intentions, in order to impart good advice, sound knowledge and practical help to all those who are in need of good advice, sound knowledge and practical help.

I must advise that this is not quite one of those books. It does, however, have certain advantages over its rivals.

If push comes to shove, it will fit perfectly into your pocket and so will not be lost on a bus or in a pub.

It is priced competitively for it is concerned mostly with the language and world of commercial theatre.

It is designed to be read in tiny chunks so as not to stretch the shortest attention span.

It is not recommended by any training course, college or academy.

This dictionary does not attempt to be in the least authoritative. It is merely a personal explanation and interpretation of our profession's words and phrases and includes a little general information that, no matter how erroneous, may be of use in the great pursuit.

It is neither word perfect nor complete. Indeed, it represents merely a part of my own take on a business that, as a Company Stage Manager, has kept me steadily amused and amazed for some forty odd years.

I hope that it may please those readers already in the profession and be some small help for all those many, many more, who, despite all good counselling, bribes and threats, are still, to coin the phrase on the cover, theatrically bent.

AA

A IS FOR

AA

Reputation being all in this business, I would seriously suggest that you pause and think very carefully before admitting to anybody that you are in any way connected with this organisation.

We all know and understand that it is indeed of great positive benefit for many thousands of people in other professions, similarly as tense and insecure as ours, and that we should only applaud that it has kept them all going as it were on their personal straight and narrow roads.

However, common knowledge that you belong to it may also prejudice your peers against you and it can become a disadvantage should the cork pop, so to speak, and the time arrives for you to phone in to let all know that you're having a 'minor breakdown' and won't be coming in to work.

You'll get less sympathy than you feel you deserve, especially if they know that your membership includes Home Start.

ABELARD AND ELOISE

It's always very useful when mixing in theatrical social circles, to have names to quote at your fingertips or, failing that, on your tongue. Two names are always better than one but you don't have to start your list with Laurel and Hardy or end up with Ant and Dec.

Double acts have been around for yonks and are especially effective when opposite sexes are teamed together. Should said opposite sexes fall in love so much the better, and better becomes even better, and particularly popular, when these liaisons are doomed, yea doubly doomed.

Anthony and Cleopatra, Tristan and Isolde, Lancelot and Guinevere, Rodolfo and Mimi, Romeo and Juliet, Bonnie and Clyde, Sid and Nancy – the doomed list is theatrically endless.

A good duo to remember is Abelard and Eloise. These star-flossed French lovers' affair was as hopeless as a Pâté de Foie Gras Diet and they had a particularly nasty fate. Not only were Abelard's balls cut off and

1

Eloise bricked up in a cellar, but they suffered a further indignity when their story was turned into a musical.

Their poignant stage tale not only had as short a run as their affair but was known dismissively throughout the business as Gobble Hard and Have a Sneeze.

ABSINTHE

Between you and me, a rather insipid drink but one that's somehow got itself associated with decadence and green fairies. You're bound to be offered it sometime in your career. Take my tip and stick to something stronger in the way of cocktails.

ACCOUNTANTS (theatrical)

You may presume that accountants, as with other moneymaking ventures, run the business of theatre these days. This is not quite true, though many accountants may believe it to be. Gone are the days when their profession was deemed as exciting as a dry fish slab on a wet Monday in Macclesfield. Recently, the profile of accountancy received an enormous fillip with *The Producers* and renewed self-confidence has resulted in some of the bolder calculators conducting singing audits. Though tone deaf, they are nevertheless charming, obliging people and, thanks to autosuggestion and hidden hypnosis, wonderful with figures. They really haven't got a clue as to what the rest of us in the theatre get up to, so please don't tell them.

ACNE
(see Makeup)

ACOUSTICS

It's terribly important for an audience to be able to ear a play no matter how vital the theatrical contribution of great mime artists, even if most of them are now either sadly dead or deadly sad.

The Victorian and Edwardian theatre architects got it right, for their clever use of horsehair and plaster meant that a theatrical whisper could be helped across the footlights and travel to the back of the gallery. In truth this was also because acting lungs had been expanding since the

Medieval Mystery Plays. Maximum velocity and volume reached their pinnacle on 5 May 1910, but on that day the sudden tragic death of Edward VII caused a rapid decline to set in, both in vocal projection and sound architectural knowledge.

My advice is to always carry a printed copy of the text whenever you attend a play. Thus prepared, if Act One has been a sonic quagmire, you can enjoy Act Two from the comfort of the stalls bar and even, when enlightened, refreshed and realising that the text is utter bilge, hurl the volume at the cast, author, or passing architect.

ACRONYMS

Theatre has a long relationship with acronyms, those words formed from the first letters of other words and usually standing for something jolly important or meaningful. ABTT (upper case) for example, stands for Association of British Theatre Technicians while rsc (lower case) for rowdy stage carpenters. Acronyms are an essential part of the backstage mystery and so you will find several more lurking on future pages.

ACT DROP (an)

Is these days seldom seen in commercial theatre. An act drop curtain, to give it its full title, is a specifically show-related front cloth to top and tail an act instead of using the house curtains.

I have seen act drops that, like book dust jackets, were often better than their contents. That may partly explain their current unpopularity with producers, apart from the sheer awful cost of making them.

ACTING AREA (the)

Is that part of the stage where the actors perform although their interpretations are not limited to this specific area. Many manage to carry on to and from their dressing rooms while others are not afraid to take their parts into the auditorium when they fall off the stage.

ACTOR MANAGER (an)

Is now that rare species of a performer – an actor prepared to produce plays; and therefore one who not only gets to play all the best parts but pays others to play the worst.

ACTOR PROOF

A part so brilliantly written that not even the worst actor in the world (see *Awards*) can ruin or destroy it. This, of course, is a perfect example of a theatrical myth.

ACTORS
(see *Performers*)

Consider and remember these two facts before you turn eagerly or uneasily to the letter P.

Firstly, even if you do not want to become one, you will still have to meet, mingle and make merry with many, many actors during a theatrical career. That is *unless* you are single-minded enough to try to carve a solo living, which as my friend Davide whisperingly confides, "Is still possiblo in Il Teatro delle Voci Registrate, Palermo, Sicily."
Secondly, actors are now of both sexes, in that they must be called 'actors'. You should only use the term 'actress' when referring to one long gone or when quoting what the proverbial said to the Bishop.

ADVANCE (an)

Is, of course, a posh term for a sub, i.e. money often lent by harassed company managers and seldom returned without threats of grotesque and horrid physical violence; i.e. 'I'll breathe on you, Bitch.'

ADVANCE (the)

Is the amount of money taken at the box office for a show's future performances. This can be split into the daily advance and the total advance for the run of the show.

The retreat is not part of the theatrical vocabulary. If a show is so bad that an entire audience asks for its money back at the interval, they haven't a hope in hell unless it's a matinee. All box offices close nightly no later than thirty minutes after curtain up.

ADVANCE BARS

One needs balls of steel and grim determination to make it to advance bars. These are positioned high above the auditorium just in front of the proscenium arch and are used to hang lamps and speakers. Please don't be tempted to swing on them no matter what their load bearing is.

Their supporting cables pass through holes in the plastered ceiling and this plaster is generally as old as the theatre. It doesn't like its routine disturbed and like an elderly relative is inclined to suddenly drop off and upset the inheritance of those working below.

ADVANCE MAN (the)

Not an actor's expression for a gullible company manager but a long-gone job description for an employee of a touring management who would precede the show from town to town, drumming up business by the use of any local publicity and large drinks for the box-office staff in their respective locals.

AESCHYLUS

This ancient Greek lived between 525 and 456 BC and between fighting off the Persian invasions at Marathon and Salamis found time, inspired by the god Dionysus, to write some ninety plays, seven of which, including the *Oresteia*, survive today.

He is most turns' forgotten hero for it was he who devised the revolutionary use of a Second Actor in plays, so that the First had at long last someone to act with rather than bouncing his monologues off disapproving chorus lines.

If Aeschylus is regarded as the father of Tragedy, his death heralded black comedy and helped inspire the development of the theatrical wig industry. He died when an eagle dropped a tortoise from a great height onto his bald head, mistaking said head for a rock.

AGENCIES

This refers to Ticket Agencies. Ticket Agencies or Agents are in the business of selling tickets.

Some sell more tickets than others, while others sell tickets for more than some.

In fact, sometimes, they do get a bit greedy. This can become an issue for you when your show is 'hot'.

If you're loitering in the foyer it's always advisable to avoid lobster-coloured families in matching shell suits screaming that they "'aven't paid ninety pounds a pop to sit in the upper circle, mate". If you should get caught, never give your name and wave them in the general direction of the Front of House Manager who will have done a brisk course of 'audience restraint' at a Health and Safety seminar.

Once clear of them you should not hesitate to personally phone the agent in question and, in the strongest possible terms, insist that you get a full share of the mark up.

AGENDA

An industry keyword meaning delay, as in, "A pay rise? It's on the agenda."

AGENTS

What do agents do, dear reader?

Ask 95% of their clients and they will respond with a single loud collective shout, "Bugger all!" adding, with a collective whine, "Apart from taking our bloody, hard-earned money."

Now, before you are tempted to immediately abandon your future 'onstage' or 'backstage' career and become an Agent, please take heed. If you choose this path, I feel it my duty to warn you that the road that lies ahead is not necessarily some smooth, yellow-bricked fantasy. It could well turn out to be but a broken, mud-stained cul de sac, both dim and dangerous.

Like the hosts of Hell, agents are legion. There are supposedly thousands of them out there, busily collecting their commissions. But, as a wise old CSM once quietly confided to me (even if it was after midnight and a case of Latvian lager), "Have you actually ever *met* an agent, my boy?"

It got me thinking, you know... thinking hard; I knew I'd certainly talked to them on the telephone hundreds of times, but met one? And come to think of it, even their disembodied voices are slightly strange: metallic or sibilant, or just plain camp.

"There are more things in Heaven and Earth, Horatio, than are dreamt of in our philosophy," so I for one stayed on this near side of the curtain.

AGGROPHOBIA

You may not find this word in other dictionaries but when you say you're suffering from this condition most of your fellow stage-workers will give you a wide berth. Always useful when you wish to avoid a dull and dreary day's rehearsal (see *Understudies*).

AL FRESCO

Should you be offered a job al fresco be sure to pack an umbrella. For, as sure as Puck, you'll be dozing halfway through an open-air production of *A Midsummer Night's Dream* when it all turns wet.

AMATEUR (an)

Is sometimes scornfully defined in this business as someone who works for nothing. This is both unfair and untrue. After all, there are many professional actors who get paid for a job but also work for nothing. It would be better to say that an amateur treats the theatre as a pastime rather than a profession, but then again it could be argued that there are many in the profession who treat it as a pastime firstly too. Perhaps it would be best to simply remember where the word comes from; from the Latin, *amator*, meaning lover, and a lover can love the theatre for both the play and the pay.

AMOROUS PROPENSITIES

If, like Samuel Johnson, your amorous propensities are readily excited by silk stockings and white bosoms, then you've chosen the right profession to get stuck into. Do remember, though, that mounting an entire production can be quite an exhausting business, so don't be alarmed if you occasionally fall out of the saddle.

AMPHITHEATRE

Not many of us nowadays can boast of employment in this type of theatre – vast, circular, open-aired and never very popular with lions or Christians.

However, should you wish to 'embroider' a sparse CV with this credit it would be authentic to locate your work on *Not Now Nero* in the Latin amphitheatrum or better still, the Greek amphitheatron.

ANGELS

Are not only the people Robbie Williams used to sing about. There is another kind, those eternal optimists who for a variety of reasons put their hard earned or ill-gained cash into a producer's production.

They are very hard to recognise in the streets of the West End for, like you and me, they wear ordinary clothes and you won't find them hanging around rehearsal rooms (not unless nudity's involved).

Any sensible producer takes very good care to keep them well away from their productions until the Last Moment, a.k.a. The First Night.

Then, if you're quick off the mark, you might have a chance to spot them. During the interval, search out the furthest, dustiest recesses of the stalls bar and you will come across a crowded, roped-off area. If no one's looking, duck under the rope and mingle, for you can be sure that those ashen-faced men and women sobbing quietly into their Veras, are angels who have just realised their investments have gone with the wind.

ANGST

A useful word to loudly emphasise when attending interminable production meetings of any Nordic drama and in need of a toilet break.

ANNOUNCEMENT (an)

Not the sort of thing you read in your local gazette's *Weddings and Deaths* and *Let's Be Social* sections, but what you may have to say many times in a stage management career.

Announcements are preferably done with a mic (see *Mic*). This way you can be heard but not seen by the audience and so avoid possible physical violence.

Don't take this personally; its not that they hate you, but when you have to go out front all hot and bothered and crave their indulgence because the *X Factor* star of the producer's choice has passed out or away or both before the show's even started, they can get a bit narked.

Luckily, auditorium seats are (mostly) secured to the auditorium floor but in my time I've oft been booed and once had to beat off a barrage of ice-cream cartons, though I suspect that they were demonstrating about the price as much as about my announcement.

Remember – never throw anything back (see *Health and Safety*); even a booster cushion can traumatise.

Luckily, your more usual type of announcement will be of this variety:

1. "Good evening Ladies and Gentlemen" – substitute 'afternoon' if it is indeed so, though I find 'evening' more refined and makes the shows go quicker.
2. "Welcome to the So and So Theatre" – always a bonus to get the name right even if some of the audience are indifferent to such detail.
3. "May we remind you that the taking of photographs is forbidden ('*verboten*' if you are doing *Cabaret*) and please turn off your mobile phones."

And you can bet even odds that one night as you begin the last part

4. "At this evening's performance the part of... will be played by..." your own mobile will ring out loud and clear.

Basic Rule: Don't answer it.

ANOUILH (Jean)

Jean was actually a man and a very good French playwright. Although dead and rather out of fashion, a useful name to drop when asked about your commitment to EU Art when you're up for that European tour of *Daddy Cool.*

ANTHEM

A lovely song from *Chess* by Tim Rice and Abba but not to be confused with…

ANTHEM (the National)

Which, to avoid any further confusion, is *God Save the Queen* and not *Rule Britannia*, no matter how many times that's sung at the Last Night of the Proms.

It is British in origin and any French claim that it was composed by Lully to thank *Dieu* for the healing of King Louis XIV's anal fistula should be briskly dismissed as *Merde*!

Some patriots attribute the tune to Purcell, but a version of the lyrics, to an arrangement by Thomas Arne, was first definitely sung in public in the presence of King George II at the Theatre Royal Drury Lane in 1745.

Bonnie Prince Charlie, on a rather successful tour with his Jacobite Army, was playing Manchester that night and threatening to transfer to London.

The spirited rendition so cheered up the Hanoverian monarch and his claque that it was encored repeatedly throughout the evening and by the 1780s had been adapted as the official British National Anthem.

As our Empires grew (see *Stoll Moss*) so did the Anthem's fame.

Towards the end of the 1900s it was so synonymous with patriotism that it had become standard practice to play it at the beginning of theatre performances.

By the 1980s, however, the Anthem was in trouble. It was no longer quite the novelty number it had been; worse still, theatres had lost their resident orchestras and the number of resident pianists employed and still able to stand by curtain up was miniscule. It was decided to quietly end the tradition except when the House of Windsor attended Gala performances. This was tactful, for it meant that the late Queen Mother could still turn on occasion to Marvin Hamlisch and say, "They're playing *our* song".

Nowadays there are three main problems whenever the Anthem is required:

1. The orchestra haven't the sheet music at hand; Jimi Hendrix doesn't play pits these days and no one else will busk it. The end

result is that a frazzled MD spends hours writing out the parts, and it's not until he picks up the baton that he realises he's put them in the wrong key.

2. No one can remember much more than the first two lines. As the full Anthem has three verses – the fourth one about "Rebellious Scots to crush" is only sung at cabinet meetings; and your ears are assailed by Gods and Queens in heathenish proportion.

3. Only those of the artificial hip and joint age know for certain that one stands to sing the Anthem – or try to. Their spontaneous efforts to get up can cause coarse confusion in the smartest auditorium. Whole rows of concerned people trying to help them to the toilet, while those less concerned urge all to sit down, shut up and listen. The end result is that many fail to rise at all to the occasion and those few that do are sadly only on their feet by the time it's all over, Ma'am.

ANTIGONE

A 20th-century play by not only the French *auteur* Anouilh and the German *Stückeschreiber* Brecht but also by Sophocles, which goes to show that most plots are as old as Ancient Greece.

ANTIPODESTA

A specialist variety act meaning a forward bender rather than a back bender. Catch them while they can and if they do land on your feet, please help them up to theirs.

ANYTHING GOES

A jolly good shrug-off expression to be used when catching grossly ill-matched members of your company in grossly compromising positions (see *Parties/between matinees/sheets/engagements*).
It's also a fine musical by Cole Porter.

APACHE DANCE

It's an expensive jaunt these days if you want to catch an Apache dance. You'll have to fly into and then around arid Arizona to find one, but the original, the real thing was really dirt cheap and more than dirty in the Paris of the 1900s.

This four-legged violent contretemps originated in the *bals musettes* of Montmartre and basically consisted of a hard man giving a hard woman a hard time.

Timing in fact was all, for each slap had to synchronise with the harsh chords of an out-of-tune accordion. It was an immensely popular act, being that the original dancers really were the real thing, but as with most forms of popular entertainment (see *Bedlam/Tyburn/Pam's People*) good taste muscled in and what was once authentically dirty was quickly sanitised, cleaned up and pretty soon, not too much in mass demand.

APRON (the)

Is a rather dated word used by equally dated stage managers for the stage area in front of the House Curtain. In Good King Charles' Golden Days (see *Restoration*) the apron was much bigger than it is today and filled with ripe bosoms and heaving oranges.

ARIA

Comes from the Italian word for air and is the posh opera expression for a song or melody sung by an individual. Please note that if he or she succumbs at the end it is not known as the 'Die Aria'.

ARMOURY

Few theatres have such things these days except for certain Art Centres in the more deprived cities of Great Britain. If you are not based in a riot zone and have the sudden need for an executioner's double-sided axe, try the National Theatre, Bapty's or your local Bert the Butcher.

ARRAS

Is not only a small town in Picardy, famous as the birthplace in 1758 of Maximilien Robespierre, but also a tapestry of the type hung on ancient walls. There is a Jacobin link here with the Bard, for in 1602 Shykespeer had his hero Hamlet thrust a dagger through an arras which thereby despatched the hidden Polonius.

The stage directions of the Folio do not tell us where the fatal blow should strike but it does lead on to the next important phrase.

ARS VINCIT OMNIA

The Theatre's motto. Please spell it correctly.

ARSE

(a) (see *Bottom*)

(b) Licking. This will get you anywhere but not necessarily everywhere.

ARSEHOLE

You can bet your bottom dollar you're going to be called this at sometime in your career and usually by somebody to whom you've refused some piddling request. Think in advance of some good ripostes: the wearied variety – "It takes one to know one" or, the dignified – "No thank you."

ARSENIC (an infusion of)

It's an old-fashioned remedy for old tiresome members of this profession, but a very effective one, even though it's slightly hard to come by these days.

You may well be tempted many times to administer a dose, but before you do so please remember the novelty of its use today may still not guarantee immunity from arrest and prosecution.

ART (1)

That's what we're all about and what's all about us if you get my meaning. Not only is it the title of a very good play but it's also got its own Government Minister so that makes art terribly important.

Art is also a collective word, and you should be aware that it comes in many varied, complex forms which can frankly, between you and I, sometimes 'do your head in'.

We are never allowed in this business to deny art because the belief that we are creating a three-letter word makes up for all of those common four-letter words used so often to describe our noblest efforts.

To enter into the spirit and essence of art you will need quite a good smattering of background knowledge to play the game, as it were.

Let's start with basic art – art as practised by artists.

Throughout the ages artists of varied skills have dabbled in Theatre. For example, in recent times such diverse talents as Lancaster (Osbert), Rhodes (Zandra), Conran (Jasper) and Hockney (David) have designed sets and posters. Even Picasso (Pablo) and Utrillo (Maurice) turned their hands to paint the odd backcloth or two.

It is when you couple up the word with another that the subject becomes a veritable Hydra: Abstract Art, Botox Art, Burlesque Art, Conceptual Art, Deco Art, Dramatic Art, Existential Art and Fuck Art (as some actors have been known to shout, coming off stage after an eight-hour production of *The Jarrow Hunger March*).

Enough. I think that even though I may not have not covered Art in its entirety, the artistic point's been made. Please heed one last warning: It's a three-letter word so, like the IRA, quite explosive.

ART (2)

Garfunkel. A popular American singer with great hair.

ARTHUR

A Great British king's first and only name and one once often used by some Great British comedy actors in humble homage to his legendary stand-ups at the Round Table. For example:

ARTHUR Askey

ARTHUR English
ARTHUR Howard
ARTHUR Lowe
ARTHUR Mullard

Though all of the above have now sadly shuffled off above or down below, the name is still superbly represented by ARTHUR Smith and it is immortalised as the title of a comedy film starring Lorna Luft's sister and the late Dudley Moore.

ARTIC

Not that centre of the frozen North suffering from typographic global warming, but an abbreviation for 'articulated lorry'. These lorries are forty feet or more in length and are the standard type used to transport all the components that make up a touring show from town to town. They are driven by large, patient men who never let you down. That task is solely the reserve of the lorries.

ARTISTE

Not the genteel way of spelling the word, or for that matter a misspelling, but the correct if antiquated way of describing a performer in the world of Variety. It made them sound posh even if their landladies knew better.

ARTISTIC

An enormous ranging, descriptive adjective encompassing the whole excitement of the creativity of theatre.
It can also be used for a very good putdown of performances and plays of a feeble, fey nature.

ASBO

An ASBO will not necessarily bar you from practising your new career but it's one of those qualifications probably best left off your CV.

ASHTRAYS

Are still sometimes come across in elderly auditoriums, screwed loosely
into the backs of decrepit seats and smelling ever so faintly of stale
Players. Health and Safety may have made their function redundant but
the word itself continues to be used to this day as an appropriate slang
term for a theatre's boxes, for these are not only of similar shape but are
usually in no better condition than the real things.

ASIDE (an)

Is a scripted spoken thought by an actor and is used usually to convey his
real feelings to the audience, e.g.:

> Actor: "And how is your sweet little Chihuahua?"
> Aside: "Stuffed and on the mantelpiece?"

ASM

Odd initials perhaps, you may think, and the truth indeed is that the
definition of these particular three letters can sometimes encompass some
rather odd people.

After an absolute *Götterdämmerung* of a play's last rehearsal, an
unkind director of my acquaintance screamed that these initials could
only mean 'Anti-Social Morons'.

It wasn't until the end of the short run and the longer last-night party
that he changed his opinion. This time he really upset those initials, still
vaguely upright, by declaring loudly that they were decidedly one and all,
'Assorted Small Members'.

Nevertheless and albeit, in the true theatrical sense, I can now reveal
to you, if you don't know, that these letters actually stand for: Assistant.
Stage. Manager.

It's a pretty vital role and deeply relevant, and our theatre world is
perpetually full of them, for they are to be found on every show ever
staged.

Please remember this mantra:

An ASM is essential,

Two are common,
Three a luxury, and
Four means that the stage manager can organise that odd night off (see *Float* and *Self Embalming for Beginners*).

With that fundamental truth established, you must also understand that though thousands start off as ASMs, thousands more finish.

It is only the talented or lucky ASM who becomes that rare caterpillar which will gloriously metamorphose again into the gaudy magnificence of the DSM butterfly (see *DSM*).

The early fall-out rate is frankly appalling. Dozens are simply lost on their very first solo journey between the warm cocoon of their local drama college and the blasted heath of their first professional interview.

Do, however, remember one stark fact and, if you are a potential ASM, take heart and draw comfort: NO show can do without you according to page 43, clause 6.2.1 of the Equity Agreement.

So, if shows have to have them and employment's possible, what on earth do they do?

Well, they do all sorts of very useful things. They carry clipboards, wear steel-capped boots, and are permitted to even physically touch actors when necessary – and sometimes, where not.

As a CSM, SM or Actor, you will have to learn to turn a blind eye (see *Nelson*) to some of their other more idiosyncratic behaviour patterns.

Why? Because although their youthful enthusiasm may well be as unprofessional as your very own conduct at spontaneous after-show happenings (see *Behave!*), they do have a certain advantage: ASMs video *everything* on their mobile phones, know how to play back the bloody things and post them regularly on Facebook.

ASPARAGUS

Should you, as an ASM, be asked to supply a soft edible prop for the show you should avoid providing the cast with this delicious vegetable (hot or cold). Sadly, many actors (warm or frigid) worry at the best of times and as some are ignorant of the effect asparagus has on their urine's odour, the induced hysteria may mean that you're going to waste considerable time in a pointless search for the whereabouts of the local STD clinic.

ASTAIRE

You will need to memorise the names of many of the legends of this business in order to acquire a veneer of knowledge when talking to your peers and also because the Job Centre may ask who you've applied to work with before they dish out your Job Seekers' Allowance.

Here for starters is Astaire.

Fred Astaire: born Frederick Austerlitz, was arguably the most influential film dancer of the last century but before his Hollywood career began, he worked extensively on Broadway and the West End in partnership with his sister Adele. Please note: Only use this example in artistic discussion, as the Job Centre may discover that Fred's last London production was around 1933.

ATTITUDE

There's a lot of that in all lines of work. It used to be a bit of an exclusive to this business but these days you're just as liable to meet it at a Prêt à Manger.

Rise above it either way, but never be caught drinking a skinny soya latte.

AUDIENCE (S)

Let's face it, however shy or misanthropic you may be there's no chance of getting away from audiences in this business, so you will have to face that fact and live with it.

Not that you will have to live with them, of course.

Audiences these days are absolutely vital for the life of a show, for gone are the days (mostly) when producers could find their backing from philanthropic simpletons who judged their production's success by the length of its run rather than by the breadth of their royalty cheques.

Audiences are also increasingly hard to find in this era of multi-entertainment. Their appearance has always rather depended on the quality of shows but these days even the best mixture of ingredients does not always guarantee their presence. That is one of the imponderable mysteries of theatre and the reason why so many one-off successful formulas are repeated in a vain attempt to jump on *The Bandwagon* – which was originally a musical revue before becoming a film.

Should any reader be tempted to have a go with that particular title, I would suggest that the only predictable guarantee is that the majority of punters for that or any other West End musical will come from Essex.

Now there's nothing wrong with that and just proves that the further east they are the further west they'll come.

Someone, a 'Jealous from Sussex', wrote to me that "Half of them seem to have a bladder problem during Act 1, and the other half hold on to theirs till Act 2."

Grossly unfair, and you may well ask, "What happens in the interval?"

The true answer, quoted to me by an erudite plumber, is a sad indictment of the sanitary state of Theatreland: "19th-century latrines are incompatible with 21st-century bladders."

And if you don't believe that, witness before the start of any Act 2 the sad, twitching queues outside that dubious sign, 'LADIES'.

AUDITIONS

As birth is to life so auditions are to theatre – necessary. So you are bound to come across them in your new career.

"What are they," you may ask, "and why have them?"

Firstly I want you to close your eyes… no sorry… this won't work; just keep on reading.

Now use your imagination while you read and picture this scene in front of you:

On a well lit stage, a long line of beautiful young women and handsome men wearing broad smiles and little else and – for God's sake, wake up! That's fantasy; here's reality:

The Time: Late afternoon
The Place: Two stuffy rooms: one filling with a steady stream of nervous actors, the other containing a solitary, very nervous actor either talking or singing or doing a combination of both while a short distance away a handful of bleary-eyed spectators gaze at him in various states of attention, from nodding off to nodded off.

Auditions are held through uncertainty. Directors and producers seldom know who will be in the show, other than possibly the leads, so they and the casting director organise auditions.

This means that a broad swathe of actors is called in to read bits of the script for the various parts.

Sadly some actors are sent along by their agents with scant regard for suitability, so you can get some very interesting interpretations which always seem to get less interesting as the day wears on.

By the time you've been through fifty actors, in the audition sense, you've been through fifty actors.

There's only one thing more dispiriting and that's when you've got a mass ensemble audition for a musical: all those looks, all those legs, and all you need's eleven, which of course refers to the dancers, rather than the legs.

Finally, do remember that if you are not actually auditioning, your initial involvement is probably to tick names off the list and gorge yourself on the lukewarm coffee and curling sandwiches. Everyone else will have an opinion, but should they ever ask for yours, the best reply is to quote Sir John Gielgud's advice: "Always cast a light Cordelia."

AUDITORIUM

Is where the audience sit in the theatre, though occasionally you'll find an odd actor out there waiting to admire his performance.

AUTHORS

Rather essential for any good play, or bad one for that matter, authors are as eternal as the optimism you will need to stay the course in this your choice of career.

Authors come in all shapes and sizes but the one thing many of them have in common is their ability to kick off. They can be really troublesome when the director decides to lose the odd comma and turn quite tedious when he tries to cut an odd act.

For many in this business there's indeed a certain truth to the old saying that "the best authors are dead authors".

AUTOGRAPH

Is not only what the demented and distressed twitching outside stage doors will want from you – and please note that if they are waiting only for your top turn's autographs, they then, on top turn's appearance, technically become "fans". Autograph is also the name of one of the most successful sound design and equipment companies in the world of theatre.

If I am slightly partisan in my enthusiasm for the firm and wish to include it as a vital piece of knowledge it is because I first worked with Andrew Bruce when he started out with Phil Clifford in the early 1970's and have done so many happy times since. The Gitanes may no longer sadly be smoked but Autograph's professionalism and pursuit of perfection still happily continues.

AUTOMATION

Is the name of the latest department to join the technical ranks of the theatre.

It's all about compressors and hydraulics and chains and hoists and its teams are staffed by people who always seem to be rolling towards you.

That's because they've spent their formative, apprentice years at sea on cruise ships. Roll with them and though you'll get a bit giddy, you'll find you can make meaningful social contact.

AVANT GARDE (Théâtre de l')

It will come as a disappointment to know that despite its origins in the City of Light, there is at this moment no theatre of that name in Paris. New, stimulating, and experimental theatre of course exists there but it seems more *arrière garde* for Ionesco's *The Bald Soprano* to be still playing the Théâtre de la Huchette ever since its first performance there in 1950.

AVOIDANCE
(see *Tax*)

BACARDI BREEZER

B IS FOR

BACARDI BREEZER

Sneered at by more spirited drinkers and abhorred by the moral minority, this lively goodtime brand of alcopops is nevertheless adored by many of your average theatre audience. It's also very useful to have a few in the fridge backstage when working on younger shows such as *Grease, High School Musical* and *Matilda* to dish out as rewards, bribes or payback.

BACCHUS

Is the Roman god of Theatre and Wine, both of which are still curiously intertwined to this very day.

BACK STORIES

There are two types of back stories in this business. The ones you will have to listen to and the ones you will have to tell.

The former involves an actor collaring you and telling you all about their two lower vertebrae both alike in agony and could you please shorten the doublet, lower the hose and get them to an osteopath.

The latter also involves an actor, one of the tedious variety, who wants to know in which hospital his or her character was born, did puberty bring on the desire to be a vegetarian, and did their present bi-polarism really stem from being part of Captain Scott's doomed expedition?

BACKING (got)

When a producer's got backing for his potential show – meaning investors – he can then get a director, a designer, a cast, a production manager, a press representative and lunches in the plural at The Ivy.

BACKING (needs)

If you hear during rehearsals that your show may be in need of backing, it indicates that some of its investors may have failed the producer's great expectations (see *Dead Authors/Out of Copyright*).

If you're told once it's opened that it's in need of urgent backing, it either means:

(a) You are not going to be paid this week.

(b) The designer's forgotten to place a flat behind the front doors of D'Urberville Hall and that the audience can see not only the back wall but also Tess and what she is up to with the crew while waiting for her cue (see *Entrance*).

BACKING FLAT (a)

A small piece of painted scenery often used with interior sets. It is placed, for example, behind an on-stage entrance so that the audience can believe the illusion that the doorway leads into a sumptuous corridor.

This belief is maintained until the unbraced backing flat topples over, the door opens and the reality of a sordid wing is revealed.

BACKSLAPPING

Goes in the same category as 'glad handing' and should only be attempted after First or Last Nights. Never backslap an actor on any other night. His wig might fall off.

BACKSTAGE

Is that area of theatre that the audience should never see but one that is essential for you if your planned career is to take off. Therefore don't be vain. Be sure to have regular eye tests and wear glasses if you have to – to see the Promised Land.

BALL BOUNCERS

You won't meet many these days except at an after-show Christmas party in the bar of a Variety Care Home. These juggling acts were popular in the 1920's but then suffered their own Depression. Please be kind but firm when the Red Bull and vodkas have kicked in and refuse their offers to show you what they can do with their balls.

BALLOON ACTS

After the rubber balloon made its first appearance in 1824 it was only a matter of time before balloon acts of all shapes and sizes would be invented. The female balloon act really took off in 1933 when the dancer Sally Rand created a sensation at the Chicago World's Fair with her novel use of transparent balloons that cost some twenty-eight dollars and fifty cents each.

Attacked by a swarm of fast-flying paperclips, the balloons were decimated and Miss Rand faced bankruptcy until help, in the shape of a transparent silk curtain, was placed between her and her audiences. Since the demise of Vaudeville and Variety, balloon acts have become very much a minority art form and any veteran performers still in the business are probably popping off as you read this.

If the ladies are no longer working the foot pumps, the skill is still represented in the United Kingdom by the Oddballs – three naked men who each naturally clutch two balloons. They are a hard act to follow.

BALLS

There are three types of theatrical balls. Those you will need in order to cope with the everyday crisis and odd dire disasters. Those you will attend in your dinner jacket or ball gown and, as the evening disintegrates, find yourself in need of the former. Finally, the third type as in 'a load of'.

The third is by far the most common.

BANANA

A 'top banana' is an old expression meaning a lead comic in a bad bunch.

The actual fruit is very useful when a play requires edible food. It can, when cut with skill, represent all sorts of meats which a vegetarian H&S Inspector would condemn within seconds if he saw the inside of the stage-management fridge.

It's also a very good prop. The great Max Miller would saunter on and start to peel one, counting the skins as he did so, "One skin, two skin, three skin…here, lady, want a bite?"

BAND CALL (a)

This applies to a single gig and is when the band and their MD get the chance to go through whatever they are due to play, rather than to go through it with whoever they are playing for. That happens later at the sound check or the show or, even later still, back at the hotel.

BAND CALLS

Are plural and therefore more expensive. If they're really expensive they become known as Orchestra Calls, for this dignified title is felt to go some ways towards justifying the number of musicians used and cost expended.

BAND PART (a)

In complete contrast to a band's parts, there's nothing mysterious, infectious or private about this item. A Band Part is a big piece of paper (size A3) on which is written the musical score for whatever instrument the musician is engaged to play.

BAND ROOM

The cast of a show are always allocated dressing rooms, but the band, if there is one, are usually given a solitary band room. Actors require many different types of rooms depending on status and numbers. Chairs, tables, even lights now have to be provided and some theatres have kindly installed showers to freeze or scald them. Band rooms are seldom so well equipped.

Band rooms are inevitably below ground in any old cellar and as close as possible to the pit entrance. Should you be tempted to peep inside you may find your face assailed by an old, smelly stage cloth or blanket, stretching from wall to wall. This partition is there so that the lady musicians can change behind it into the virtuosos or viragos they will become for two long hours.

As your eyes accustom to the lonely gloom you may also note a few broken mugs, some empty instrument cases and a collapsed sofa. Nothing and nobody else.

Don't be alarmed, for this absence is no mystery. You see, it is still a good two minutes before curtain up and the musicians are on their way in to work, finishing their pints in the pub or, if they are a dep, sitting in the pit and wondering if they're in the right theatre.

It's only at the interval that you'll literally have to elbow your way to get into the band room. That's when the lights are on, the laughter's loud and the band-room bar is open.

BANJO

If anyone tells you they haven't been seen since *Jeeves* and *The Black and White Minstrels* – a severely edited (headless) version can be glimpsed occasionally on CBBC – tell them to bloody get with it.

Banjos are HUGE in Bulgaria with their trance anthem *The Sun Has Got His Fez On.*

BANK

A bad word, I know, for so many of us these days, but the fact remains that you really do need to have a bank account in this business. That's because nearly all salaries are paid by automatic transfer unless you're a member of BECTU and insist on cash, which can be dangerous, especially if your locker is of the kind found in many theatres, sans lock, sans key and of course, sans door.

Company Managers are sometimes spotted leaving stage doors 'for the bank'.

This happens more frequently on those shows where the folk they are looking after are as scintillating as Peggy Lee's *The Folks Who Live on the Hill* (see *How To Sing in a Wheelchair*).

I am sure that many of these trips are legitimate but may I suggest that it is possible that some mix business with pleasure. I can confide, for example, that until quite recently there was what appeared to be a very agreeable pub called Bank, near the Aldwych. Unsurprisingly it was called that because it occupied a vacated bank, but if you think that's just a one off, look around.

London's littered with wealth-emptied, Beaujolais-brimming vaults. Something has to be done with them; someone has to fill them.

And it could be...

BAR (a)

You are mistaken if you think this is only something that you lean against when trying to put off your inevitable decline and fall. Bars are used by the stage and electrical departments to hang cloths and lamps. They are made of hollowed metal, attached to lines and are flown in and out as required if the theatre has a grid.

BAR BELLS

If you ever visited a theatre before picking up this book and your conversion, (see *On the Road: Damascus, Derby, Droitwich*), you may recall that, having waited to be served for ten minutes at the sticky end of the Dress Circle bar, you were just about to quench your thirst when an irritatingly loud and tinny bell started to ring. This may well have made you dribble your drink over yourself or your companion, but its main intent is to remind you that fun's up and it's time to get back to your seat.

Don't despair. Bar bells always start to ring a good five minutes before the curtain is about to rise.

They are also rung so that you will be tempted to order another 'quick one' to take back to your seat or gulp another down again in one. Either way the theatre wins. Bar profits are maximised and bar staff are rewarded with whatever's left on the counter. Don't be rushed. Enjoy those full five minutes and when you do make your return, you'll probably find that Act Two has already started and that allows you, undetectable in the dark, to move to a much better seat.

BARD (the)

Is, of course, the Bard of Avon (Stratford-upon) known alternatively as:

Christopher Marlowe;
Francis Bacon;
The Earl of Oxford;
Queen Elizabeth;

Edmund Spenser;
The Earl of Southampton;
The Earl of Derby;
Sir Walter Raleigh;
Sir Philip Sidney.

BARNDOORS

Are seldom shut in theatres, no matter what the weather. These four flapped masking devices fit in front of Fresnel lanterns and are used to shape angles and to mask spillage.

BARRE (a)

The simple explanation that a barre is a piece of timber used by dancers to warm up only creates the further mystery of how on earth do they?

The answer lies in the thighs.

Dancers have well-developed thighs. Their superb adductors longus, brevis and magnus have been known to reduce balletomanes to jelly. With hardly any effort, they are able, by the use of their well-turned knees, to ply their thighs in a beautiful upward or downward motion and so warm up those wonderful muscles lurking beneath the surface of their lovely legs. The piece of wood, or barre, is there for them to hold onto with one hand and so allow them to make fluid, elegant and graceful hand gestures with the other. Without a barre, of course, they'd fall flat on their arses.

BASSO BUFFO

And that's what you can call a basso profundo if he too should fall on his culo.

BASTARD PROMPT
(see *Prompt Corner*)

BASTINADO

A form of torture favoured by the late Inquisition, not used these days though referred to frequently – "What an absoluto bastinado of a performance" et cetera.

BATON (a)

Is the thin white stick which some unashamedly short-sighted conductors wave, point and throw at their orchestras.

They are very expensive items so please return any you should find to their maestros. They may not thank you but at least, once reunited with their sticks, they will have less chance of falling under a train at Covent Garden.

BATTEN

Is another term for a type of bar, the difference being that battens are made of wood. These days they are mostly found in elderly theatres with restricted budgets and are full of splinters. You may curse them as you extract yet another ancient sliver from your thumb. But please remember that they are a memento from a golden age, part of our theatrical heritage and at the end of a season make very good firewood.

BATTERIES

Are everywhere in theatres, especially musical theatre. If you are gadget-orientated these can be very useful for your radios, razors and rabbits, and are always freely available from the Sound Department (the batteries, that is).

BAY (a)

A bay is an area in the dock of a theatre, a space where scenery can be stored, hence the term 'scene bay'. It's important to remember that the bay's in the dock and pay no heed when you hear Otis Redding going on and on and on about the dock of the bay.

BEATS WORKING

A standard phrase used by most in the profession as they watch *Doctors*. However, even if you have got a long-running show to do, you still don't have to do a day's work in a year.

Look at it this way – there are 365 days in the year. Say you average 6 hours at 'work' a day. That's a quarter of a day which comes to 1.75 days a week. Now there are 52 weeks in the year so that makes it 91 days. But, you don't work Sundays so that brings it down to 39. Your annual holiday entitlement is 28 days, knock off Christmas Day and take 10 days off sick on full pay as you're entitled to under Equity rules and… Do you see what I mean?

BECTU

Are the initials that stand for the Broadcasting Entertainment Cinematographic and Theatre Union. All backstage departments with the exception of stage management, sound and automation are represented by it and use its rules and regulations on an everyday working basis.

BEGGAR'S OPERA (the)

One for the theatrical fact bank as it's regarded as the first British Musical. It dates from 1728 so you don't have to claim to have been in it. Score points, however, by mentioning that you're considering mounting *Polly*, the sequel not seen since 1771.

BENDER

You may argue that going on a bender is less a theatrical expression and more of a national pastime. However, in this profession the word has a specific stage meaning – a bender is a contortionist and, specifically, a backbender, one of whom you may well become when you're out on one.

BIBLE (the)

The truth that God is a forgiving sort of chap is well illustrated by the fact that, on a daily basis, technical departments in a theatre somewhere in the UK, put together their alternative Bibles and are never struck by lightning. These Bibles contain all the information about their departments. They are assembled with reverence and care, printed and bound and then put away in drawers where most are eaten by plagues of locusts.

BILL (a)

Is the original name for a theatrical poster. Georgian and Victorian playbills were similar to bills of fare: long, elaborate printed lists of attractions with the tastiest turns at the top. While bills for plays had by the end of the 19th century evolved into lithographic illustrated posters, bills for Music Hall and Variety remained pretty much the same in appearance till the expiry of those types of entertainment.

Audiences liked this information format. Reading up from the bottom, if they were so inclined, they could tell which artist was on when, and so knew exactly how long to stay in the bar before catching the star attractions. These headliners would always be at the top of the sheet hence the expression to 'top the bill'.

BILL (the)

They may be universal, but there's one variety that strikes terror into all who work in the theatre, be they charge hands or castrati (see *DIY/Scissors*).

Its arrival marks the death knell of any company meal. It always exceeds your calculation. It is never indicative of what you have eaten and drunk and, frankly, should be evaded whenever possible.

However, don't think you will be alone in trying to avoid the moment of reckoning. Occasionally this subterfuge turns into what is known as the 'The Great Escape'.

I once saw the whole cast of a production of Molière's *L'Avare* tottering away from a restaurant, struck down, so they claimed, by mass 'food poisoning' – an extreme reaction – they had only opened their menus and seen that it was £9.99 for the prix fixe.

Indeed, theatrical appetites being what they are, it's a pretty rare event. It's far more common, as the pudding is being munched or the port slurped, for you to feel occasional hands, other than your own, grasping your thighs, ankles or other extremities.

Don't flatter yourself. It's only one of the tighter members of the cast, making a groping exit under the table towards the door.

On the other hand, do flatter yourself and join them. You might get a free meal twice.

BILLING

Is the position of an actor's name on a poster or any other publicity medium that advertises the show. Top billing means exactly that and if the actor's name is above the title you know that you are lucky enough to be working with someone whose agent believes is a star.

Negotiations for billing can take longer than any other form of contractual negotiation and can sometimes lead to frosty relationships between fellow actors. I did know a chief electrician who for a small reward from one actor would tamper with the neon letters on the theatre's marquee spelling his rival's name.

But that was years ago, in a literate era. These days you're lucky if the tytles write.

BILLY BLOCK

Is not an early Benjamin Britten opera. It's just a pulley on a short length of rope which, indeed, could be the opening line of a late lyric by Roger Rougher.

BIS

Absolutely essential for the fuller briefcase: a Bladder Irrigation Set will raise your status in any company. And there are social possibilities. Even the most tight-fisted actor will be unable to resist purchasing you a drink just to see whether you will have need of the BIS before Last Orders.

BISHOP'S FINGER (the)

Not only a splendid ale but also a potentially lethal prop from the days of dangerous theatre.

As invented and worn by the Lancastrian tragedian C.D. Hesketh, it had a sad tendency to get the last laugh in *Murder in the Cloisters*.

Twelve inches long and fundamentally unstable, any sudden, hasty dramatic gesture would send it sailing high into the stalls to land on or in an audience's head or eye.

BIZ

A keyword of the profession. Never forget (that's another) that you're now in the business of show (see *Accountants/Mangled English*).

BLACK (a)

A descriptive noun for a hanging leg or border.

So, when you hear the command "Hang the Blacks!" relax. You're safe, for you're in that most tolerant and unprejudiced of all environments: the theatre.

BLACKS

Are the name and colour of the clothes worn by all inherently professional people backstage apart from certain dressers who prefer to flaunt their semi-toned torsos and lallies as naked as they can. Ignore them. You've seen it all before the night before.

BLADDER (a pig's)

Used to be widely used backstage for the sound effect of screeching brakes, kettles and sopranos. Nowadays it is only found in non-EU imported pork pies so if your director still insists on authenticity for his production of *The Ghost Train* or *Stuff Dame Nellie In The Teapot*, you will probably have to buy a gross to guarantee any chance of reassembly.

BLOCK

Nothing to do with drains, I'm glad to say. To block a show or the cast means to plot the movements of the actors around the stage as they speak their lines. This usually happens at the beginning of rehearsals and, if the director has done any homework, means that said actors will enter wittily through doors, pace the stage and not fall directly into the orchestra pit. That will happen later.

The blocking of a move is written down by the DSM in the Book so that when the director and actors are arguing about motivation or unmentioned upstaging, the actual line that makes them leap to their feet to kiss, kill or top each other can be pinpointed for clarification. That is, of course, if the DSM has written it down legibly, or even for that matter, at all.

BLOW (a big)

An orchestral term describing a challenging score arrangement with a lot of top notes that will take the brass section several pints to master and several more to recover from.

BLUR

If an actor tells you "its all a blur", he's either:

(a) Going blind
(b) Forgotten his contact lenses
(c) Been on a blinder the night before

BO (1)

Body Odour is bound to challenge you at some time in your new career. Not so much these days in Musical Theatre as it used to, due to EU regulations, but the occasion will arise when you will be forced to act or risk a general revolt by other members of your company.

My advice is to splash out, buy some Lynx and to hell with the expense.

BO (2)

Stands for a theatre's Box Office, which is where the public come to buy, pick up or exchange their theatre tickets.

BO (3)

Stands for Black Out (see *Blackout*). That's when all the lights on stage go out suddenly and that's down to a deliberate artistic decision or a power cut.

BO Number 1

Is the Box Office Manager. He or she will have a Number 2 under him or her, a Number 3 and possibly a Number 4. That's, of course, if they can all squeeze into their tiny boxes.

These 'front line' stalwarts not only have to put up with the public, they also have to put up with producers, who are generally acknowledged to be trickier than the public. Box offices are seldom praised. If a show's doing well they're taken for granted and if it isn't, they sometimes get more than their fair share of stick.

So, from me, a hearty thank you to you all, and yes, I will have another small glass...

BOARDS

When someone tells you "I'm about to tread the boards" always remind them to put their shoes on first. Stage-floor surfaces, like battens, are full of splinters and some have holes large enough to completely swallow and mangle the largest toe.

BOAT TRUCK (a)

Is nothing more than a platform on wheels to enable the scenery built on top of it – such as a gondola for *The Gondoliers* or a ship for *The Pirates of Penzance* – to glide smoothly across the stage. That, of course, is the theory. In practice, the execution, as Albert Pierrepoint pointed out, is not necessarily so.

BOHEMIAN GIRL (the)

If the *Beggar's Opera* is regarded as the first British Musical, *The Bohemian Girl* is cited as the forerunner of the modern musical. It was first performed at Drury Lane in 1844 and since then has been produced all over the world and into this century.

The show's most famous song is "I dreamt that I dwelt in marble halls" though personally I prefer Stan Laurel's line from the 1936 film, "Well blow me down with an anchovy."

BOMB

Al Qaeda doesn't have a monopoly on this word, for it is used in our business as well, i.e.: "The show bombed on the First Night."

Harassed producers may cast the critics as the perpetrators of such outrages, but one should always remember that bad shows more often than not self-destruct.

BOOK

'On the Book' is akin to 'on the piste' because you can't get off it until it's over.

The Book itself is a very battered manuscript that the DSM guards with dogged ferocity. However, if she or he should succumb to one of the many theatrical illnesses (see *Off*) it's your responsibility.

Open it carefully. On one side of the page you will see the printed words of your show and on the other you will note numbers, stains and squiggles. These, if deciphered, relate not only to the actors' movements but more importantly to when the lights come up, the revolve moves, the bridge descends et cetera.

It's very important for the success and safety of the show that all these vital movements are cued in a right and timely manner. So take my invariable advice: Hand the Book over immediately to your ASM.

BOOK (off the)

Means that at a certain time in rehearsals the cast collectively throw away their scripts and rely on their retentive memories to speak their lines. This occasion usually coincides with what is called a 'Stagger Through' (see *Stagger Through*). After that ordeal's over the cast really do have to rely on their retentive memories as they scramble to find where they tossed the playwright's finest.

BOOK FLAT (a)

Doesn't mean a volume-lined garret near the British Library but a pair of stage flats hinged together which, when opened wide, can be self-supporting. I say 'can' because being opened too wide can also lead to discomfort when they fall on top of cast and crew.

BOOM

Sang Charles Trenet but not with that spelling nor in any theatre near you. You may, however, find booms in the plural on each side of the stage or in the front of the proscenium – vertical metal bars on which are attached lamps. The lamps themselves are attached to horizontal brackets called boom arms which for safety are sometimes chained.

BOOTH (a)

Can be either front of house or backstage. If it's in the former area it will usually be a neat, functional open box accommodating the sound or lighting desk for a specific show. If located in the latter, it will be generally far less sartorial. The backstage variety are coarsely roofed and ramshackle in construction – any old spare flats lashed together will do the job – for their usual function is their use as a quick change area.

Of course, these attempts at privacy make them far more sociable areas.

But it is when a quick change becomes a vocal booth for off-stage singing that the party really starts.

BOOTS

Not the chemists, but in theatrical parlance the different types that are worn on and off stage.

We can dismiss the 'On Stage' lot, they're mostly all about twenty miles from London and still no sign of Dick, or they're of the Jack variety as worn by Sturm und Drag at The Blue Max, Wapping, and certain lantern-jawed directors.

What you need to concentrate on, if you are not an artiste, are the steel-capped variety.

These stern beauties are worn by technicians for Health and Safety reasons. The trouble is, though Health and Safety may miss you by a mile, the boots certainly won't if you're within a yard of their vicinity.

Stay well clear to avoid horrendous chiropody bills.

BORDER

Refers to neither Break for the Border, a long gone, watering-hole located in the depths of the Palladium cellars, nor a singular short-lived bookshop but a simple piece of dusty black tat. This can be of varying length and if stretched horizontally in the air from one side of the stage to the other will conceal from the audience all sorts of things which hang from the grid (see *Grid*) e.g. lights, scenery, flymen, et cetera, et cetera...

BOTTOM

If an older actor asks if you have ever seen his bottom, don't take offence.

He is probably referring to his performance in the *Dream* at the Mincinghampton Festival of 1985.

If he isn't, it's probably best to leave the dressing room.

BOUNCE THE TABS (!)

Is the shouted command meaning that, at the curtain call, the house curtain should not stay down at the end of a company bow but should immediately rise so that said company can bow again and again and even, again.

It's not a order you'll hear often these days from the grim lips of a grizzled stage director. This is due to the sad facts that it can only be done manually, flymen aren't as strong as they used to be, and nor for that matter is the applause. Lastly, besides those cautions, there is the constant danger of venerable house curtains disintegrating under the strain of such violent exercise.

BOWS (the)

Is another word for the curtain calls though not always an accurate description of what happens. Some performers categorically refuse to bow to unresponsive audiences whilst others, in attempting to, pass out and have to take what is technically and correctly called a horizontal bow.

BOX SET (a)

A box set comprises of a number of flats cleated together with the required doors and windows inserted. The whole gives a realistic impression of the interior of a room. That is until an actor can't get through the door and pushes the flats over.

BOXES

You will find boxes in most theatres on the left and right sides of the auditorium. They are ideal for those members of the audience sporting only one eye and you will find that this specific type of visually impaired viewer is usually quite happy to sit in them. However, it can go badly wrong if he or she is sold a box with their bad eye, as it were, down wind.

Boxes are also useful for intimate trysts during backstage parties; however, you must always remember to use an Upper Circle box, otherwise you could be filmed and compromised from the very same.

BRACE

Not only half of something to help the way your trouser hangs but an essential piece of wooden theatrical equipment designed to hold up and steady a piece of scenery called a flat.

There are variations such as a French Brace and, of course, the Human Brace.

This is when an ASM gallantly takes the place of a misplaced or forgotten brace. The correct posture is arms and legs outstretched akin to that Leonardo da Vinci drawing.

Make sure that the Human Brace is encouraged to lean slightly *backwards* for this will prevent the flat from falling *forwards* onto the actors.

BRAIL LINE (a)

Is generally a length of sash or rope used to keep flying pieces in an unnatural position. This position is paradoxically necessary because it stops them from interfering with other flying pieces going quietly about their business.

If that concerns you, I suggest you do not become a flyman.

BRAVO

That's what audiences are meant to shout at the end of a dramatic evening in appreciation of a dramatic evening. I even think I've heard it myself a few times in my career, but that could be balls.

BREAK A LEG

Is one of those reverse expressions employed on an opening night as a good-luck greeting. It has its origins in America, dating supposedly from the assassination of President Lincoln by the actor John Wilkes Booth.

Booth is said to have injured his leg as he leapt from the Presidential box onto the stage of Ford's Theatre. It is seldom used in the UK, except with true and literal malice at the Royal Ballet.

BREAKING INTO THE THEATRE

You will have to do that often once you have. Getting your first job may be terribly difficult but it's nothing in comparison to the problems that will face you when the stage door's locked on a Saturday night.

You've left the iron on, the wig box blazing, the fridge open, your wallet on the worktop and your house keys God knows where.

I've always found the best way in is up and over, for fly-gallery doors are often left ajar for ventilation. However, a word of caution: be careful as you ascend and *always* look up. That way you will avoid colliding with colleagues breaking out.

BRECHT

Bertolt, though dead, is still the most influential German playwright of our times. His name is always worth slipping into a heated Marxist discussion and his lyrics to songs such as *Mack the Knife* are quite cutting edge.

BREL

Jacques Brel – *chanteur, composeur et acteur* – ranks as one of the world's most famous Belgians alongside the equally memorable Tin Tin and Poirot.

His song *Next* is the perfect retort to sing back at angry auditionistas who won't stop in mid-song and leave the stage.

Sadly, though, even his greatest fans now have to accept that the title of the musical based on his chansons, *Jacques Brel is Alive and Well and Living in Paris,* is completely out of date.

BRIBERY ACT, 2011

There has been much recent discussion regarding this new Act of Parliament. I do not believe that it will have much impact on the theatrical profession as producers' First Night gifts seldom make any difference to performances and are next day generally returned to the pound shop (see *Receipts, retention of).*

BRIDGE (a)

Is not a bridge too far unless the set designer's millimetres have been interpreted as centimetres at the scenery workshop.

Bridges are not just solid pieces of scenery but can also be raised electrically or hydraulically. They are sometimes lowered sooner than either of these methods when the full chorus of the *Der Fliegende Holländer* clamber aboard.

BRINGING DOWN THE HOUSE

When you hear a comedian or actor exclaiming that he brought the house down he is not necessarily referring to a small personal failure at DIY. He may mean that his routine or performance was an absolute triumph.

Although that's the perceived understanding of the phrase, it is not quite correct.

The saying entered our theatrical vocabulary during the Golden Age of Variety when any audience worth their salt (see *Condiments*) could watch a whole show for one and sixpence while drinking an endless glass of stout. This steady damp consumption made them quite picky about what they watched.

After all, a vanishing camel hump is a novelty act only once. To get those punters even out of the bars needed something rather good, and to bring the house down and back to their seats, someone really special.

It happened, of course, but if that someone really special didn't live up to expectations the house would not only come down but pelt the poor sod with their empty glasses.

BROKEN SINKS

It's a mysterious fact to outsiders that there are more broken sinks in old theatre dressing rooms than in any other type of communal building. The explanation is quite simple: this is because such dressing rooms were never open-planned.

They have stout doors that can either shut and lock, or lock and shut.

These offer welcome privacy in a very public, stressful workplace and allow their tense occupants and guests the chance to sink to sin and, in so doing, of course, break the sink.

The extent of breakage stretches from hairline fractures to gaping holes, depending on who is doing what to whom.

BUDGET (a)

Could be described by some cynics as an imaginary estimate for a necessary expense or, indeed, as a necessary estimate for an imaginary expense. It's really all a matter of what it's for. Budgets pop up in every area of theatre when putting on a show.

They're needed so that each department knows what's affordable, though that has seldom deterred over-spending. The man who has to vigorously police budget control on the front line is the Production Manager. A hard job, so go out of your way to buy him a large Prosecco but don't forget to get a receipt for both of you.

BULLSHIT

You won't get away from it.

Now, I'm not talking of the type found in some blood-stained sandy arena south of Seville. That type you can *completely* avoid as long as you don't go to Spain.

I'm talking of the verbal bullshit your ears are going to have to put up with throughout your new career.

It's unavoidable because *everybody* you work with is going to be giving you a mouthful of it at some time or other. Don't let it get you down. The answer to bullshit is simple – bullshit back.

Actor: Really sorry I'm so late. You won't believe this! My train didn't stop for me. There we were all shouting and waving and the bloody driver left us all standing on the platform and...

You: Holy Shite! You're the lucky one! I was one of the poor sods on that bloody train. The brakes failed. When the driver died we all had to jump for it at Clapham Junction so, before you ask, that's why I'm limping...

BURNT SUGAR

When budgets are tight, it's best to use burnt sugar mixed with various degrees of water to simulate drinks as and when needed in the action of the play.

You can, by careful measurement, make whisky or wine look completely different but, of course, both will taste really awful. The actors will complain but stick to your budget. That way you can have a nice Chardonnay to sip each evening at the end of the show.

BUS AND TRUCK

An American technical term for interminable tours of at least a date or two per week.

As all the company travel and sleep on the bus, you'll have to bed your dates on the truck if you want any privacy.

BUSINESS

In theatrical terms means not only the amount of money a show pulls in each night but also what actors can get up on stage. It could be clearly instructed in the script but, more likely, it's what the actor invents himself to put his costume, props or body to true and full advantage. His business can be amusing for the audience but quite baffling for other actors for such business tends to be conducted upstage of them, and they will never glimpse those inflatable trousers, stuffed chickens or knobbly knees.

BUSK

If you're told to 'busk it' don't bother to search for your harmonica. It means that there hasn't been time to rehearse the final scene change when the express train crashes through and into the dining hall of Branson Manor. You can in this particular instance, of course, refuse to busk it but, peer pressure being what it is, you may well end up on stage or, for that matter, on the OP wall. Whatever transpires, do wear a hard hat.

BUZZ

If you hear a buzz at work it could be one of two problems:

(a) It's your ears
(b) It's the Sound Department

A cotton bud, if firmly inserted, should fix either.

CADENZA

C IS FOR:

CADENZA (a)

Is not some Neapolitan speciality that can be ordered at Pizza Express. If it could, it would be stamped with a Government Health Warning.

Should you be standing in the wings and a singer informs you that she's about to *have* a cadenza, drop down fast and low. High-pitched screaming hysterics can do irreversible damage to eardrums.

Should the same turn *do* one on stage it means you are both working in an opera and she is exercising her self-imposed right to embellish her part, show off her vocal technique and sing your socks off. Not necessarily a pleasant experience but perhaps preferable to her embellishment of your own part.

CALLS

Are announcements put out over the tannoy in the corner to the company telling them both the time-honoured obligatory calls (see *Half*) and personal courtesy calls put out once the show has started to inform the actors that their time on stage is fast approaching.

Actors have great faith in these calls as they can turn the show relay off and watch their televisions undisturbed by the sound of other actors droning on and on and on.

If, as sometimes happens, the DSM should forget to put this type of call out, you will soon hear the traditional live sound-effect of running footsteps. These will be accompanied by angry raised voices from the stage repeating lines that with familiarity lose all their dramatic meaning.

After the panic come the recriminations: (a) Insist the call went out; (b) Remind the actor that it is purely a courtesy call; (c) Duck.

CAMP

Is a word always difficult to describe and often misunderstood. It is usually compared with 'butch' but that restricts it to the purely physical. It's deep rooted yet flimsy, sometimes androgynous and always robust.

Its application depends above all on a person's perception of life and humour, be they comedian or audience.

To broadly illustrate this: Frankie Howard was camp, Sue Pollard is, Ricky Gervais isn't.

CANDLES

Are not allowed to be lit backstage. They can be lit on stage but only in the presence of a fireman, so remember to make sure that he is as inconspicuous as possible.

CARBON TETRACHLORIDE

A very effective dry-cleaning fluid but I would not recommend it, as several of my late heavy-smoking friends did, 'to clear the old pipes'.

CARETAKER (the)

Not the play by Harold Pinter, but the person you may meet when you open a creaky rehearsal room door for the first time. If he is wearing full slap, a wig and is dragged up in a Salvation Army uniform be assured of getting a nice cuppa tea and a ginger biscuit.

CARPETS

Most theatres have robust, wee-maintained carpets in all their main FOH areas. This is to soak up any moisture brought in by the public and so prevent patrons slipping on rain-water, spilled beverages or worse.

Backstage carpets are different. The sensible rule is that they should be decrepit, dirty and full of fleas and mites. Their appearance is a health warning in itself and guarantees that only the most desperate employees will suffer carpet burn.

CAST (the)

Is the collective name for all the actors in a production. There is no limit. Casts can be of any number, from one hundred down to one, and, in the case of at least one whodunit, you can end with none.

An uplifting thought towards the end of a gruelling tour, but sadly, always, only a state of mind.

CAST (to)

This verb is used as in "Mr Garrett was cast in the role of the second gravedigger but regrettably fell into the trap."

CASTING COUCH (the)

Gone are the days when a predatory producer would furnish his inner sanctum with a casting couch in order to sexually abuse any young, hopeful actress who might come knocking at his door in search of fame and fortune.

Modern office furniture just isn't up to such robust antics, so these days such appointments with Destiny, or whatever her name is, are usually in Quality Inns.

CASTRATO

All the rage in the 18th century, but these days this type of singer just hasn't got what it takes. It's tenor this and tenor that and if they really want that high note, the powers that be in Opera will bend their budgets for a countertenor.

CATS

All theatres used to have them to keep the rodent population down, but nowadays they're judged a bit of a health hazard themselves so you won't see so many of them around. Not unless the Musical comes your way. And that can be a bit of a health hazard in itself, if only for the dancers (see *Fur balls/Accidental neutering*).

CENTRE / LINE

This is the measurement that splits a stage into two equal halves: stage left and stage right. It is from this line, running from the front of a stage to the back wall of a theatre that calculations are taken (see *Mark Up*) so that sets, furniture, props and even actors can be hopefully positioned correctly according to the dictates of author or director.

CHAMPAGNE

If shampoo is the traditional tipple for this impoverished profession, how, and when on earth, do we get our hands on it? Beg, borrow or steal answers the first question, and the second on First Nights, Last Nights, Anniversaries, Weddings, Funerals, Bar Mitzvahs, New Year's Eves, Birthdays, and finally, on those special Red Letter Days.

These are, of course, Mondays, Tuesdays, Wednesdays, Thursdays, Fridays and Saturdays, and, as you certainly can't pay a final demand on Sundays, treat yourself on the Sabbath to an appropriate Dom Perignon.

CHAPERONES

Are needed if you have any child actors in your production. Luckily, finding chaperones these days is no problem as their most important qualification (and may I here say 'shame' in answer to those nasty enough to say 'only'), is the lack of a criminal record. Their local authority furnish a certificate to prove their authenticity, so, once you've seen that, it's basically all over to them.

Chaperones are well worth every penny of their salaries, for not only do they have to do all the looking after of their charges, they even have to eat with them.

Above all, they will also head off a far worse peril than the most obnoxious child actor – said child actor's parents.

CHARISMA

A much-bandied word to describe a performer's ability to inspire and charm his audience. Beware of hyped imitations that have as much charisma as a night-soiled glove puppet.

CHARLATAN

If anybody calls you this, their intent is to accuse you of being a fraud. They may be cruelly accurate in their assessment but they have left themselves open to rebuke by their sloppy knowledge of words. Remind them firmly that you do not presume to know anything of medicine, are not a quack and can they kindly duck off.

CHATEAUNEUF-DU-PAPE

If it's good enough for the Pope – it's good enough for the actor.

However, try not to drink more than half a bottle a day. Remember, you've got a whole night to get through as well.

CHEQUES

Are not only old fashioned, they can also be very bad news.

You're on tour with *Smiles on Their Faces* (which is more than can be said of the audience). It's a quiet week in Sunderland – even Sid James died there – and then the Company Manager comes round with brown envelopes on the Thursday night.

This should immediately alert you. Nothing ever good comes in brown envelopes. Should you open it and find, instead of the usual bland statement, a cheque for your wages, it's time for Plan S to swing into action. Go directly to the Company Office, and borrow a sub sufficient to cover the cheque. If you get there on time, the Company Manager will have only subbed himself and there'll be enough for you. You can indeed also pay the cheque in on Friday but remember the bank of Toyland never pays out after playtime.

CHILDREN (stage)

To be forewarned is to be forearmed. Therefore it should be emphasised that where there's a chaperone in a show there's inevitably going to be a child or three.

That's, of course, unless a shameless scam is being pulled. It's uncommon to have 'phantom' children in a production, but it's always a good thing for you to count how many are on stage and then compare numbers with the programme.

A show's usually down a child or two each night for some reason or other – the infectious type such as nits, gnats or nuts (dry-roasted) or for social excuses – school concerts, outings or visiting Granny in hospital. If there are more of them off than you can handle, you should phone the nearest midget agency. Their clients are instantly available and can go on their own to the toilet, though please check that they return.

CHIROPRACTOR

Actors often need manipulation but sometimes, when words aren't enough, a bit of rough physical pain can do the trick. However, whatever the temptation, never touch them yourself. Send them to a physiotherapist (especially women), osteopath (some of whom indeed double up as other forms of path) or, failing the availability of either species, guide them in the direction of a chiropractor; they're a sort of cross between the other two and there's a good one in High Wycombe.

CHLOROFORM

Sometimes used as a solvent for dry cleaning dirty stiff collars, it is also a general anaesthetic that can explain the rigidity of some wardrobe staff on a Saturday matinee.

CHOREOGRAPHER

Is the person in Musical Theatre who comes up with all those breathless routines. Painting stories and telling tales in dance can be complex or simple.

Some choreographers have very clever arms, legs and brains. Others use other people's.

CHORUS

A Chorus is employed in both Opera and Musical Theatre.

In Opera, a chorus often comprises an enormous crowd moving jerkily but singing lustily. In Musical Theatre, it is more likely to consist of a tiny group of dancers in perfect step trying to sing tunefully.

CHORUS BOY/GIRL

An old-fashioned Musical Theatre word for a dancer and one only used now as a bit of a put-down.

These days we have a male ensemble and a female ensemble though neither title gives any clue to their dancing ability. This, of course, can be a help if they can't dance.

If a member of the public complains of their inability to do a time step it can be countered that they are employed for their singing ability. You'll get away with that, for most ensemble tracks are now recorded.

CHRISTMAS

Falls into three categories in the Theatre: Work, Cards and Presents.

The general rule of thumb is to hope for some of the first, expect lots of the second and be grateful if you receive any of the third.

For many in this business Christmas is the busiest time of the year. This is because the Panto Season guarantees work for more people in a single month than the other eleven combined. Audiences are also guaranteed, to a degree sufficient for even the flakiest producers to risk their all. It's sad to think, though, that Health and Safety may soon reduce attendances as there's nothing so satisfying for an afternoon's matinee audience than throwing sweets at the cast and vice-versa, especially if they're of the hard-boiled variety.

CITT

Is the Canadian Institute for Theatre Technology.

CLAP

Is what an audience should do at the end of a play; so, if some cocky actor comes up to you after his first entrance and says he's got one already, please refer him to a clinic.

If the play's a bummer you may have to encourage the audience yourself by leading the applause. I would suggest that you do this from the back of the stalls or circle for, by setting an example, you may shame them and even the attendants into joining in as well. Your cast will always appreciate your efforts, especially if they have struggled gallantly through an evening of appalling un-dramatic moments. But don't overdo it. Always bear in mind John Osborne's wise line from *The Entertainer*, "Don't clap too hard – it's a very old building."

CLAQUE

Not what gets removed by your dentist every ten years or so but a gang of middle-aged enthusiasts, or, as some people put it, simpletons, who follow their favourite Top Turns from show to show and shower their every entrance and exit with applause and spittle.

In bygone days they would be paid by their Top Turns for this support, but now, as it's not tax deductible, they have to buy their own bloody tickets and do it, my darlings, for lurrv.

CLAVINOVA

Sounds Italian but in fact is the creation of the Yamaha Corporation. This cunning digital piano is a wonderful asset to any show. Its synthesiser can imitate literally hundreds of acoustic and electronic instruments. This means, all importantly to those technically employed, that, if it's in use on a show, your hernias will be less aggravated on 'Get Ins' or 'Get Outs'.

CLEANERS

This may be a disappointment, but if your heart's dead set on a dirt-encrusted Marigold career in the theatre you'll have to go to somewhere in the provinces, somewhere like Milton Keynes. The truth is, if you are British, you haven't a hope in hell of becoming a cleaner in the West End and, furthermore, if you want to get any cleaning done, you'll have to speak Spanish.

Why? It's because London theatre-cleaners these days, like cocaine, come from Colombia, and are flown in several times a year on special chartered flights. I am glad to say that they are hardworking and charming and sing like cockatoos as they hoover away, for few theatres can yet afford a Dyson.

However, please note these words of warning: Remember to use the wastepaper bins and never leave any old rubbish such as reviews, wage slips or socks on top of dressing-table surfaces. Should you do so, they'll be there for years. Our Colombians, though strong and sturdy, are mostly short of stature and working regulations only ever allow 'light dusting' above head height.

CLEANING (dry)

As costumes inevitably acquire a Churchillian covering of blood, sweat and tears it is advisable to have them dry cleaned by the Wardrobe Department at least once a week. This gives you an ideal opportunity to refresh yours at no extra cost so they'll be ready by Saturday to go clubbing again.

CLEAR (to)

When the cry rings out to 'clear the stage' it is a command that must be obeyed implicitly and immediately. It is a warning that dire things are about to happen and danger lurks for those who dally.

Should you unwisely dally, you must suffer the consequences. Be prepared for Chitty Chitty Bang Bang to land on your head or to be tapped roughly in the nether regions by Hamlet and told to piss off out of his soliloquy.

CLEARANCE

This word has a ring of sensibility about it, a clean-cut resonance, a decisive command, even a suggestion of colonic irrigation.

Front of House Managers calmly give 'clearance' to backstage every night to indicate that, as far as they're concerned, all is perfectly ready in their domain and the show can now have permission to start. Whether it does is quite another matter.

The odds are that just as the echo of 'clearance' dies away, a school party, several hundred strong, will appear in the foyer. The FOH Manager will examine the seat number of one of the tickets the desperate teachers are waving about. His brow furrows. It appears that a mass double-booking has happened. "Oh Shit! – I do apologise Madam". This is the moment when things both speed up and block up.

An usher will be sent running to the box office while the FOH Manager sprints backstage to delay the show. If there isn't an accident on the stairs there's bound to be one as he sails through the pass door and knocks over several of the cast waiting in the wing.

The Stage Manager will bark for "Quiet!" The Company Manager will attempt to pick everybody up and usually lose his glasses. The

Deputy Stage Manager will knit on and put yet another call out for "Orchestra to the pit".

As injured players feebly demand the accident book, the FOH manager will state the obvious by crying "Hold the Curtain!" He will then tear off back to the front followed closely, if myopically, by the Company Manager.

When they arrive, the foyer will be empty, of course, apart from the odd usher and the Box Office Manager.

"Where...they...gone?" croaks the FOH Manager hoarsely. The Box Office Manager's lips curl into a sibilant sneer. "Gone? They've gone to their right theatre, dear."

The Company Manager will have missed that. He may be ever so slightly deaf but he's already gone himself, to start the bloody show.

CLEARING STICK (a)

Is an enormously long piece of stick, sometimes measuring more than thirty feet, which you may find resting quietly on the dusty back walls of un-modernised theatres.

Its rest is occasionally disturbed by a member of the crew who, picking it up with amazingly strong arms, will use it, not to eject something nasty from the nose of a member of the audience in row S of the stalls, but to straighten up tangled borders or stray lengths of sash which have been left dangling on bars at the fit-up.

CLEAT (a)

Is a piece of metal, shaped as a double hook and screwed at the top and bottom, into the offstage side of a flat, so that a line from the next flat can be tied to it and so secure the flats together.

CLEAT (to)

This is the practice of cleating, a highly skilled art involving the line and one flick of the wrist... or two... or three. Or ask the Master Carpenter to help.

CLENCHED

Teeth or buttocks are usually a sign that something nasty's going to happen in the wings. You'll either be asked to hold them or the actor's about to sing. Both should be avoided if possible.

CLICK TRACK (a)

Is a pre-recorded piece of music or vocals which has a constant click so that the band can keep in time with the track.

CLOTH

A painted piece of canvas scenery, usually flown (see *Flys*). It's usually positioned at the back of a set unless, of course, it's a front cloth.

COCKTAILS

No doubt you are wondering, as you may have often done before, why this word needs any explanation.

The answer is that cocktails are very important for the success of theatrical parties. This is because the profession neither hangs about nor back when free drink is on offer and it is seldom long before free drink becomes an endangered species.

How does one solve this problem of biblical ancestry?

The answer is, of course, with cocktails. All the hosts have to do is to gather up all the massed remaining dregs add crushed ice, an optional olive or slice of lemon to create concoctions strong enough to fail a CO_2 emission test.

If any of your more fastidious guests actually ask what's in them, and that's if they are by now capable of asking such a complex question, tap the nose (yours) whisper 'bartender's secret' and give them a long slow wink (gin/vodka/plum brandy/fernet branca/tequila and just a dash of yellow chartreuse).

COMING ROUND?

This does not refer to what may happen to you after a good lashing of the above item.

When an actor asks you this it's not because his performance has necessarily floored you but because he is inviting you to see him in his dressing room after the show. Then you can floor him.

COMP

Is the abbreviation for a complimentary ticket, meaning a free one.

Comps are usually dished out on Previews and First Nights and thereafter whenever the management need to impress (see *Dress* and *Paper the House*).

For the record, as far as the producer is concerned, there is actually no such thing as a free ticket, for the cost of the paper it is printed on is, of course, always charged back to him.

COMPANY MANAGERS

All shows have to have one and most people who work with them will say that's quite enough. Company Managers lead solitary lives but do occasionally meet for social intercourse. These gatherings are known as Croakings, Clusters or Covens.

COMPLIMENT

In this insecure business it never does any harm to compliment your fellow workers on a job well done. Just be sure you've got their name and part right.

CONDUCTOR

Every orchestra has a conductor. Who conducts who is another matter.

CONTINGENCY REHEARSAL (a)

Legend has it that it was a gruff touring stage director of the 1950s, George Runt a.k.a. Grunt to friend and foe alike, who created the first contingency rehearsal.

This took place on the afternoon of the opening night at the Playhouse, Edinburgh, when it was discovered that the entire village set of *Brigadoon* had somehow disappeared.

Grunt, by the judicious use of fists and threats, persuaded his dancers to assume such tortuous physical postures that they simultaneously resembled both Highland flings and Highland hovels.

Ever since then, all conscientious stage managers assume that dozens of worst-case scenarios will strike their particular production. They spend weeks, if not months, working out every possible solution to keep the curtain up. When they are satisfied at last that every possibility has been thought of, they print multiple copies of their *Great Book of Contingencies*.

This is placed carefully in each actor's outstretched hand, just in time to be thrown in the dustbin with all their other Last Night rubbish.

CONTRACT

When a Management issues you with a contract you must not think that your life is in any more danger than it already is. Nor does it give you *carte blanche* to wreak havoc on your fellow workers. One must be discreet after all, so, should you wish to go the full hog please remember Crookback's words "Why I can smile, and murder while I smile."

A contract is merely a written confirmation of your verbal agreement so, when that happens and before you open your mouth to accept, please remember the old Bolivian miners' saying: "When the Devil offers tin it will not change to gold."

CORNER
(see *Prompt Corner*)

CORPORATE HOSPITALITY

Is an increasingly nice little earner for theatre owners.

The corporate suits arrive and are met in the theatre's foyer by charming nubile attendants, or failing that, anyone with a fairly clean shirt. They are conducted to a dimly lit room and plied before the show with house champagne, the odd canapé, programmes and er... that's it.

Until the interval, of course, when for the corporate suits, a sense of uncanny *déjà vu* returns.

They're met, conducted to a dimly lit room et cetera, et cetera. The consolation for those suits who corporately never want to look back, is that this *déjà vu* lasts never more than fifteen minutes, or, ten if there isn't a dimly lit lavatory en suite, so to speak, in the dimly lit room and they have to join the rest of the queue at the back of the stalls.

CORPSE (to)

I may be presumptuous but I must challenge the *Concise Oxford Dictionary*'s assertion that a corpse can only spoil a piece of acting when an actor forgets his lines or confuses an actress while playing her part.

They may believe that in the bar at the Randolph or wherever else the editors hang out and very possibly because ghastly student corpses litter their collective Playhouse memories, but I've never known a *good* corpse to either spoil or confuse. The art of a good corpse is in the sharing.

If lines are forgotten it's not unknown for the audience to shout them out and if Mabel Mincing goes to open a door and the handle comes off in her hand, she *may* corpse but you can bet your bottom dollar that the audience *will*.

People love things to go wrong and as theatre's meant to be live, even if sometimes played by the living dead, the odds are that they will.

Hubristic actors will complain that their fellow actors or their audience "have ruined a memorable performance" and you can further discomfort them by saying that that wonderful moment of nemesis is probably all that will be memorable.

CORPSES

You'll come across lots of these in your career, and I'm afraid you're going to learn to step over them calmly when they've been removed from the auditorium to more private areas such as the Dress Circle corridors.

Mind you, you can console yourself with the fact that they are not really corpses, for people technically never actually die in theatres. They always oblige managements by clinically passing away in the backs of those swiftly summoned ambulances.

COTE COUR

The French expression for Stage Left. French actors check that they have not strayed on to the wrong side of the centre line by looking to the *gauche* and touching their *coeurs*.

COTE JARDIN

And this means Stage Right.

COUNTERWEIGHTS

These, which together make up the counterweight system, are used to fly heavy pieces of scenery. These are collectively as heavy as whatever is required to be flown, so don't ever cross them.

COVERS
(see *Understudies*)

COWARD

In this dictionary the word means, of course, the one and only Noël Coward. The Master may have passed over but he is still with us. He usually appears towards the end of a theatrical evening when the original gags and bon mots have fizzled out. Silence being one of the original sins as far as turns are concerned, you can be sure that someone will fill a lengthening pause with, "Have I told you my best ever Noël Coward story? Apparently this huge horse and..." the Master lives again. Apparently.

CRACK UP (to)

The American equivalent of 'to corpse'.

CRADLE (a)

Is the technical term for the metal frame into which counterweights are loaded (see *Flys*).

CRASH BUCKET

Not your first car, but a metal bucket into which is poured broken glass from a specific height and with sufficient force in order to create the very realistic sound-effect of... breaking glass.

CREW

Is the collective name for all those stagehands and stage electricians who work the shows and make them work. You would imagine that the days when Long John Silver would have signed them up are long gone, but I can assure you that, happily, the buccaneering spirit lives on.

If you don't believe me just try keeping up with them at a staff party – no sensible CSM ever does, or at least *never* remembers if he has tried to.

CREWED (to be)

Was a terrible fate for bygone actors. Crewe Station featured in every touring company's train journey for it was at this junction that they would have to disembark and switch carriages to carry on to Middlesbrough, Macclesfield or Muckleswick.

Should those of ancient limbs and creaking joints miss their connection, then hours or even days could go by before relief arrived. The poor sods had only soot, sparks and soliloquies to pass the time.

CRITICS

Some say critics, in the immortal words of Lionel Bart, "ain't wot they used to be".

They forget that the Jeremy Clarkson type of reviewer has also been around ever since the supposed golden days of Shaw, Agate and Tynan.

For many an editor a good headline's the first priority, indeed the only priority. A deep knowledge of theatre has never been more essential than a strong opinion. So we're lucky today to still have several critics such as Billington and Coveney who have both and can combine them constructively.

CROSS (to)

When the blocking of a show is underway and it is found that the actor must move from one side of the stage to the other in order to perpetrate rough physical violence on another, then this is called 'to cross', even if they do end up kissing.

CRUCIFIXION

Not practised much these days and only every ten years in Oberammergau.

Enthusiasts can only hope one day for *Spartacus! The Musical.*

CRUELTY

The Theatre can be a cruel workplace. Much of the cruelty is unintentional but there are those in authority who follow the Bard's direction to the letter and have as their mantra, "I must be cruel only to be kind."

CUE

Once a show has been blocked it becomes apparent to 'those who know' where lights should change, when actors should enter and why the stuffed rhinoceros should explode at that precise artistic moment.

To make all this happen in a consistent manner, cast and crew are given verbal or visual cues. These are words or actions, derived from the script, to help trigger themselves or the mechanics. To aid the need for what is often very vital split second-timing, the next items are required.

CUE LIGHTS

Should you be standing in the wings and see the glow of a little green bulb, you are standing close to what is known as a cue light, a small metal contraption, powered by electricity and the DSM's stern and sometimes stiff, if stubby, forefinger. In fact, you are now 'on standby' to do something useful either off stage or on.

So when the green bulb dies and an angry red one starts to flash persistently, I suggest you'd better make a move, for you've missed your bloody cue, matey.

CURSES
(see *Superstitions*)

CURTAIN CALLS

When Frank Sinatra sang, "and so I face the final curtain", he was, of course, referring to that moment in the journey of every actor, be they good or bad: the moment of death.

Your everyday curtain call in contrast, is all about the acceptance of applause and the celebration of life. Every corpse in every jolly Agatha Christie whodunit or gay Jacobean drama consistently beats the Grim Reaper by resurrecting themselves just in time for the curtain. And sometimes it gets quite silly and over the top. Just watch the curtain call of Gogol's *Dead Souls*.

CURTAIN LINE

That final line of dialogue which neatly brings the play to an end. However, please note that that event is totally dependent on the actor remembering his words. Failure to do so can either leave the audience in the dark or the actor himself – for board operators and DSM's have trains to catch and a 'Black Out' is sometimes kinder than waiting for a memory restoration (see *Buckingham/Congreve/Dryden/... errrr*).

CUTS

Let's get one thing absolutely clear. As a matter of principle, people in this business should never take voluntary redundancy unless they've been sectioned.

However, there is another cut that needs to be accepted by everybody in the greater scheme of things. This is a script cut. The more sensitive type of director or producer may well tell the author first in private that this or that act has to go. Or, they may not.

That's fine if they're dealing with a dead author but not so fine if he's pacing the rehearsal room.

No matter how messy that all becomes, the fall-out is nothing to compare with the carnage when an actor loses lines.

Nevertheless you can always be supportive to playwrights and fellow actors by putting on your iPod and playing them the immortal voice of P.P. Arnold reminding all of them once again that, "The First Cut Is The Deepest."

CVs

Apart from personal mail correctly addressed to yourself, your stage door will receive the occasional stamped or hand-delivered envelopes marked for the urgent attention of the Director or the Production Manager. This is a pity as neither of these worthies is seldom ever around in time to receive them. These envelopes sit sadly for weeks yellowing in a dusty recess until the stage door remembers and hands them on to the stage management. They are then torn open immediately in the desperate hope of cash, cheques or a compromising photo and then briskly dispatched to the recycling bin. This is a shame. I believe that they should always be read most carefully.

Some people say a Curriculum Vitae is seldom worth the paper it's written on.

Don't believe them. Many CVs I've read over the years have contained glorious mistakes and breathless lies and, once turned over, make very good notepaper to scribble an anonymous reply in kind.

CYC

Stands for cyclorama. A tight-stretched cloth or gauze at the back of a set on which lighting designers create sunrises, sunsets and all the other visual needs for *Fiddler on the Roof* et al.

DAME

D IS FOR:

DAME

There are two types of theatrical Dames: Those that appear every Christmas and those that appear at the Olivier Awards.

To avoid any confusion, the former are mostly men and the latter mostly ladies.

DANCE CAPTAIN

In the constant battle to maintain a show's standards the role of Dance Captain in Musical Theatre is, as the title indicates, an important one. In association, or more usually, in the absence of a resident assistant choreographer, the Dance Captain pores over charts, plots and maps to work out who in the cast can fill in the gaping holes invariably caused by holidays and sickness. If the ranks are very thin, he or she will gallantly fill both breach and track. It's not an easy job. Some fully deserve the title of captain while others would be better ranked as lance-corporals or bombardiers.

DARK

If you hear whisperings that a theatre's gone dark, it hasn't become any more haunted than it already is, but is temporarily closed as there's no producer available to rent the decaying pile of crumbling bricks this week.

DARLING

Should be used as a name when suffering from sudden memory loss.

You can address both sexes of actors as 'Darling' with no offence taken.

Remember, though, that some theatrical etiquette lingers. Never, ever address members of the theatrical nobility as 'Darling' unless you're in bed with them.

DBO

Are the initials for a 'Dead Black Out'. Sadly, an everyday occurrence for many people in this business, even if it usually happens after midnight.

For those of a more serious and sober nature it is alternatively when the board operator plunges the stage into utter darkness to end a scene. It is also used by some opportunistic and priapic actors to begin one.

DE WINTERED v DEWYNTERED

In more robust times naughty leading ladies on some shows were occasionally De Wintered by jealous, vengeful producers. This entailed the branding of their lissom shoulders with a red-hot iron in the shape of a *fleur de lys*. Nowadays this ghastly practice is just not on for most producers are less into jealousy and vengeance and more into profit. Therefore if their current show has been Dewyntered it means that they have wisely entrusted the marketing of their production to the experts. Dewynters have conceived the posters, images and public conception of over a thousand shows. British theatre marketing is in general continuously robust but this company have set benchmarks of creativity, and if you doubt me, just think *The Phantom of the Opera, Les Misérables* and *Cats*.

DEAD

A dead is a technical term. A flying piece, such as a cloth will have a top dead, usually so that it cannot be seen by the audience, and a bottom dead, meaning that that is as far as it should be flown in. Any further in, and casts could suffer decapitation.

DEAD LIST
(see *Offs*)

DECK (the)

Is another word for the stage floor. If it sounds rather nautical this is because of the strong connection that existed in the 17th century between ships and theatre. By that I mean the mutual use of compatible equipment as well as "Hello Sailor".

In America, a 'deck hand' is the equivalent to our charge hand. Note the nautical tie-in again though it is unlikely that the first American deck hand arrived on the *Mayflower*. Hitting the deck does not refer to tiny tantrums but indicates that a cloth is in or that turns are dancing up a storm.

DENTISTRY

An expense that's just about justified by the Inland Revenue. I am afraid, though, that it is only allowable for actors and other Equity members. This unfairness explains why audiences occasionally panic when they first glimpse the Front of House Manager's un-reconstructed smile.

Actors' teeth are always a problem. There's more shoring up of root-canal work going on now than ever before, which to my mind only confirms that the great days of Ferdinand De Lesseps are well and truly over.

The good news is that fixatives are much stronger than they used to be. In the last decade I've only heard of two sets of dentures actually landing on the stage, and one of those was coughed up from the orchestra pit.

DEP (a)

Nothing to do with Johnny. This stands for those shadowy technicians, ASMs and musicians who suddenly appear in place of one (or all) of your salaried employees to do their jobs, while the people they are depping for are doing someone else's.

The majority aim to please, but if they don't and as they invoice, you never have to worry too much about paying them.

DESIGNER (four types of)

You will meet four categories of designers in the Theatre:

Set Designer
Lighting Designer
Sound Designer

Costume Designer

Quite often the Set Designer doubles up as the Costume Designer and that's why in some shows you can't tell the difference between the curtains and the costumes.

However, it's a theatrical truth that all four categories, with the very odd exception, are brim full of lovely people who understand instinctively the difficulties their designs bring to everybody else. It's a measure of their artistic integrity that they don't give a damn.

DETAIL

An eye for detail is vital in this business. It's not something that comes naturally. However, with rigorous practice and self-tuition, within time you'll be able to realise when half the cast are missing from the stage at curtain up.

Once you've soared over this hurdle the sky's the limit. That there are no boundaries to detail is best illustrated in a delightful story told by one of the West End's ticketing coordinators, the great Edwin Shaw.

In the days when a typical number one panto could number twenty sets and a hundred actors, children, animals and others, the producer Prince Littler came to Sheffield to see a matinee.

He stood happily at the back of the stalls until the moment arrived for the final walk down. One glimpse and he stormed into the manager's office in a fury.

"Axminster!" he raged at Edwin. "They've put Axminster on the treads. In my shows there's only one carpet fit for a walk down and that's a Wilton. Get It!"

'Get It' was and 'It' was there and laid by the second show.

DIE (to)

Actors are said to die, not only when you read of their passing several months afterwards in *The Stage*, but also when they fail dismally in their performances.

Overall, I do believe the latter is the sadder, especially on a matinee day.

DIGS

Are where you stay on tour if your credit card been rejected at the local Holiday Inn.

These digs are lodging houses and were once exclusively theatrical. Few of them still are and few of them are still around. So, should you find one, you will have to share with all sorts of other desperadoes and the level of thoughtful care and kind consideration that was extended to Sir Matthew Fluffit's Company of Players has slipped away over the years.

You can still occasionally expect to get a cooked breakfast at some digs (one egg, boiled or bleached) but those evenings are long gone when landladies would leave a nightly cold collation wilting for you in the lounge.

For that matter, as most landladies have gone the way of their collations, you'll be spared the excitement of those damp nylon sheets and faulty gas fires and exploding boilers and have to make do with some dull hotel with damp nylon duvets and faulty central heating and exploding toilets.

DIM and DIMMER

Are not only your stage electrics department's equivalent to *Dumb and Dumber* but also two key electrical words.

To 'dim' means to bring the lights, both in the auditorium and on stage, down in intensity but never so much as to endanger anyone attempting to leave the auditorium to relieve themselves nor to encourage them to remain seated and so soil the auditorium.

The actors on stage are of no concern. They are used to working in the dark. Many of them, at some point in their careers, will have spent bewildering weeks in confused attempts to interpret the more oblique verse works of Jude Le Tenebreux. Most are also up for groping in the dark but, of course, that's a directorial decision.

A dimmer is the actual piece of equipment that reduces the current in a circuit and so creates a dim to whichever degree is required to create an appropriate lighting state.

DINNER JACKET

You'll need one for First Nights but don't worry about the trousers. Everyone's too busy searching for a famous or a friendly face to look below the waist.

DIPSOMANIA

Should be avoided before lunch.

DIRECTOR

A widely used term for those responsible for overseeing the artistic creation of a show but who are sometimes not responsible for the artistic outcome.

DISCIPLINE

Is essential in others but a CSM doesn't set examples. A CSM is one.

DISTRESS A PROP

You will never make an inanimate object cry, but you can distress an Argos toaster with enough sandpaper and paint for it to pass from the front as the prototype invented by Da Vinci in 1497, for possible inclusion in any future reworked revivals of *Leonardo the Musical*.

DL

Stands for Down Left.

DLP

Means Dead Letter Perfect and refers to the ability of that near mythical performer who can correctly remember every word of his part and retain them in his memory bank for the run of the show.

DOCK (1)

Yes, we've all ended up in there, haven't we? But, for those of us both in the biz and out on remand, the Dock also means a dark, abandoned area of a theatre, with huge, wind-rattled doors that open onto a dingy side street or alley unused apart from when a show's getting in and getting out (see *Get In* and *Get Out*). It's a very useful place to blow off a temper tantrum and have a quiet fag. Or vice-versa.

DOCK (2)

There may come a time when as Company Manager you have to dock actors but you won't need a pair of scissors except in the unlikely event that they're paid in cash.

DOGS

Shaykespear, as always, got it right again. "Let slip the dogs of war," he versed and the results to this day are always bloody chaos! Notice that I'm not talking Dog. That's singular. Most lonely hounds can be persuaded to sit and even not to bark. BUT, put them together and they'll follow their nose, or anything else they fancy. Always remember too, that proven mathematical certainty – the more dogs on stage the greater the mess.

DONKEYS

Are not often seen on the professional stage, with the notable exception of the rarely performed *Don Quixote*.

However, if you are desperate for a sighting of them, they, or at least their tails, can be glimpsed in the occasional nativity play.

DOOR SLAM (a)

It was the custom years ago for a rep theatre to have a small, though perfectly fitted, upright door as an integral part of its stage equipment.

This was not for those actors of restricted growth unable to reach the normal height of a knob or handle, but so that the stage management could slam or open it to their hearts' content to produce the sound-effect of a real door opening or slamming.

Apart from this trick, a firmly attached knocker could add further realism, as could a rattling chain or two, heavy bolts and, for that final touch, some light squeaking from female ASMs to indicate creaking, dry hinges in desperate need of lubrication.

You might well ask why all this couldn't have been done on the actual doors of the set, and the answer is, of course, that they'd have probably collapsed.

Besides that, you should remember that, even today, unless your builder has been really skimping, few real kitchen or lounge doors lead directly onto the street, so these door slams set in the wings added a touch of further and often much needed realism to *Murder at Gore Grange*.

Nowadays most sound-effects are digital, but should you come across one of these door slams standing forlornly in the dust of the dock, treat it with respect. Rusty nails lead on to tetanus.

DOUBLE (a)

Is sometimes simultaneously in evidence on both sides of the curtain.

There's the Grey Goose variety that the creatives who have flown in for the show dip into and sip as they watch their creation from the back of the Dress Circle.

Then on stage there's the double they're viewing, for though the composer has demanded singing identical twins for his version of *I Due Gemeli Veneziani*, not even Jedward are available.

It is when the creatives see two conductors sawing through the Entr'acte that it's high time to revert to a single.

DR

Stands for Down Right.

DRAMATURGE

Not something you step on in the wings but a 'specialist' in theatre drama, specialising in script editing and play analysis.

DRENCHER (the)

Sometimes it's best to be cruel to be kind so I must state, "Incompetence is all around us in the work place."

That's why it's absolutely vital that all should know where the drencher lurks and never, ever touch. That's unless you really want to get soaked, and that fetish could and should get you the sack.

The drencher is always right next to the iron (see *Iron*). Climb the stairs to the wardrobe. Go past it and onto the fly floor and if you peer through the shadows you will see its shape running across the whole top of the proscenium arch.

That's where the perforated pipe is, but its controls are much easier to reach and so are far, far more vulnerable. The lever to release the water into the pipe in case of fire is generally in the prompt-side wing by the prompt corner. It is protected from casual touch by a frame but it's not foolproof. So, should you see some idiot fiddling with it, tell them to back off straight away or you'll all end up in *Singin' In the Rain*.

DRESS

A dress is, of course, something that actors wear on or off stage, but when used as a verb its meaning is to make up the numbers of an audience by giving out comps.

It also can mean moving the audience skilfully around. Not, of course, by yanking them to their feet by their coats and collars but by upgrading those in the cheaper seats to best stalls or circle. A house that looks full encourages both actors and audiences whereas an empty auditorium asks the inevitable question: "What are we doing here?"

DRESS (the scene)

This can happen after the director's had a jolly good lunch and decides that one of the things needed to make Mark Antony's speech in the Forum more dramatic, is a larger crowd of Friends, Romans, Countrymen. The result is that any actors not 'on' in that scene are used to beef up the Citizens, until it's pointed out that Brutus, Cassius, Cinna, Casca et al. are rather too recognisable.

On the other hand, when you are all embarked on something that's bound to end in disaster – say that car crash of a musical, *The People's Princess!* – it really does make sense to dress as many scenes as possible.

Pile everybody on as guests at St Paul's and then on again as paparazzi in Paris and the audience will be too busy working out why the Queen Mum is bopping away in both locations to worry too much about lyrics such as "We'll be Bo Peep if you'll be Wayne Sleep".

DRESS (the set)

When your show's essential working props have been collected, discarded and distributed its time to 'dress the set'. This usually happens on a standing set, and care must always be taken to place only appropriate items in keeping with the time, atmosphere and location of the play.

Thus it would be incorrect to have a working television set in the corner of the trench in *Journey's End*, no matter what round England's through to in the World Cup.

DRESS CIRCLE

Is a lovely shop near Seven Dials in London where you can get every show-related CD or DVD that has ever been released should you be so inclined.

If you're not, it's that part of a theatre's auditorium directly above the stalls.

DRESS REHEARSAL

The Dress Rehearsal is the final rehearsal before the production is viewed by the paying public. As befits its name, the cast are fully costumed and everything else needed to complete the overall look and sound of the piece, down to the very last screw should be working, in place and ready to go. That's the theory but not always the practice.

Please note that theatre people take seriously the old adage that "a bad dress rehearsal heralds a good first night".

With that in mind, don't be surprised when the leading man falls into the pit, the revolve jams, the lights fade and Milady's wig bursts into flames; it's just every department hedging their bets.

DRESSERS

Can be Welsh though this is never thought of as a handicap.

Dressers look after the actors' costumes and sometimes the actors themselves, if the latter bother to tip them.

They are of all ages and sizes and their backgrounds range widely, though nowadays they are most commonly young, out-of-work dancers waiting for a job, or old, out-of-work dancers doing one.

DROP (salary/glitter/dead)

Drops in salary should be avoided from the moment you have agreed and signed your contract. They never prolong the life of a show and are a clear indication of its imminent demise.

Glitter drops happen at the end of musical 'spectaculars' when clouds of shiny, tiny coloured strips of paper cascade down from the grid onto the stage.

These should also be avoided for they are exhausting to sweep up night after night and who really wants to fall out of a grid?

So, stick to your principles and avoid dropping dead.

DRUGS

Are not encouraged in the workplace.

DRUIDS

I'll have you know are avid theatregoers. This fact cannot be disproved as few are prepared to don their ceremonial gowns outside their sacred groves.

DRUNKS

These days are more likely to be found in the auditorium than on stage. This is because all branches of our profession take their work far more seriously than they used to. They are dedicated to their art, aware of their responsibility and lack the facility of a backstage bar.

Not so the audience. From the moment they cross the portals they are besieged by temptation and instant gratification. It is to the credit of the present moral stance of theatre owners that bar prices are so high that immediate intoxication is well nigh impossible.

It is also a credit to the intelligence of most of the audience that they recognise this stark fact and responsibly purchase only soft drinks and tonics to take into the auditorium so they can mix them with their own bottles of chosen spirits in the comfort of their seats.

DRY (a)

Can be a possible consequence of thirst; however, it would unwise to accuse an actor of forgetting his lines because of a hangover unless you were out drinking with him the night before. More likely, a dry is the consequence of boredom, or repetitious mental strain or even early dementia and should be dealt afterwards with delicacy or drink, but only ever after the show. For instant relief see *Prompt*.

DRY ICE

Not only what fills your glass in some poncey cocktail bar but a stalwart and veteran bit of theatrical magic.

It gives the illusion that billowing mist and fog are out and about all over the shop, floor and blasted heath.

Dry Ice is, in fact, nothing more than a block of carbon dioxide. When said carbon dioxide comes into contact with warm water (H_2O) it produces a low-lying haze effect which occasionally, is pushed in the right direction to create this stunning effect. QED.

DSC

Not the Distinguished Stage Cross awarded for theatrical gallantry under appalling reviews, but the initials that stand simply for Down Stage Centre.

Down Stage Centre is the area where most leading actors like to stand, quite alone and in front of only you... you, their admiring audience.

That's if they are quite alone. If there are other actors dotted around them and a scene to commence, then you're far more likely to spot them Up Stage Centre leaning nonchalantly against a doorframe or two, engaged in animated dialogue with those other actors who now find themselves Down Stage Centre and whose faces you cannot see.

DSL

Down Stage Left. The opposite to DSR.

DSM

Doesn't stand for a Dead Stage Manager. It stands for that miracle of resuscitation – a Deputy Stage Manager

Now, I must explain that that position's one up on an Assistant Stage Manager but, and this can be really muddling, one above a Stage Manager.

Why the confusion? Well, it's all because DSMs are rather like birds. They like to roost.

They're at their happiest and safest on a perch high above every initial's heads where they can get on with what's called 'Calling the Show'.

Only those in direct communication can hear what they actually call it, but suffice to say most descriptions are pretty vile. Besides that they also get on with useful hobbies such as applying makeup and reading *Heat*.

Twitching admirers should never stand directly beneath their perches. Dropped eyeliners can be deadly.

DSR

Refers to Down Stage Right which, of course, is dependent on a DSC and directly opposite from DSL.

DUCK

Not a nostalgic reference to that quirky, quacky show *Ducktastic* at the Albery Theatre but the traditional cry heard on stage when a flying piece comes hurtling in on the wrong cue. Never question the authenticity of this order, for should you do, you may hit the deck just that fraction sooner than the scenery.

EAR

E IS FOR:

EAR

This isn't as commonplace as it sounds. Everybody, barring those mutilated by a foreign rugby pack, has a pair, but you have to be gifted and also in the biz to have 'an ear'.

This means you can identify, react and even keep time to the deep complex subtleties of the Status Quo songbook.

EARLY

As a conscientious member of this profession you should always be early for work, even if you do find yourself incredibly lonely.

EASY

Remember this: Nothing is in this game.

EATING

Is an essential part of your work life and a corner stone of your social skills (see *Meal Breaks* and *Using a Knife and Fork*).

ELEPHANTS

Never encourage the use of elephants on stage. Adequate dressing-room facilities will not be available.

ELSINORE

As everyone should know, is Hamlet's castle.

Hamlet always causes passionate debate amongst actors: i.e. "Does he sleep with Ophelia?" "Never" "Yes" "Only on tour".

But you too can now contribute by explaining calmly that Elsinore (with an 'e') is really Kronborg castle in Helsingør which is just four kilometres across the Øresund from Sweden's Helsingborg which, of course, has its own Konserthus and by that time everyone will have calmed down and drifted far away.

ENEMA

Highly recommended for tight-lipped actors having temper tantrums.

However, never, ever administer one yourself. It's a messy job so leave it to one of those qualified First Aiders or, failing that, your Wardrobe Master. They've always got a spare hose sticking out of their twin tub.

ENO

Are the proud initials of the English National Opera who are collectively based at the Coliseum in St Martin's Lane, London. They also stand for three essential parts of anybody's equipment who wishes to work in this business: Ear, Nose, Orifice. Please note that, though I use the singular noun in each case, no mutilation is required for entry.

ENT

Stands for ear, nose and throat. Specialists in the treatment of these areas of an actor's anatomy are to be found mostly in Harley Street, London, though there are others, of course, outside the capital. They are seriously professional and seriously expensive but for both producer and actor their advice can be expensively serious to ignore.

ENTERTAIN

A mantra of our profession ever since Baby Jane piped out the immortal song, 'Let Me Entertain You' in *Gypsy*.

ENTR'ACTE

Is really the most annoying moment in a Musical's interval for cast, audience and orchestra alike.

It is when the conductor taps his baton on the head of his lead violin and briskly starts the regurgitation of the highlights of Act One and the next to come.

The cast have to stop editing rival Facebooks and dash to the stage.

The audience, spilling their interval drinks for which they've waited at the bar for fifteen minutes, have to stumble to their seats.

The orchestra, with the exception of the lead violin, have to leave the pub.

ENTRANCE

An actor makes his 'entrance' by circumnavigating all the hazards offstage to arrive in one piece and on two legs, both on stage and on time.

EPK

Stands for an Electronic Press Kit which comprises clips from a production on DVD or Digi-Beta for broadcast use. An EPK is widely used these days by managements as a producer-friendly tool to help market their shows. One big advantage is that the actors on it look their very best no matter how early in the day or late in the evening it is screened.

EQUITY

Isn't just a voice-activated phone line. British Actors' Equity is the actors' trade union and if that sounds slightly social, it really does try to help all those who can't always help themselves and need help in this hard-nosed business.

To prove this point it provides probably the most expensive pocket diary in the world.

ESTA

A defunct anonym only to be used to win quiz nights as the Entertainment Services and Technology Association has now merged with PLASA – the Professional Lighting and Sound Association.

ESTONIA

This plucky little nation's theatrical credentials don't stop at the Eurovision Song Contest.

According to reliable sources, eight hundred thousand Estonians out of a total population of one and a half million attend a theatre every year, which puts our attendance record as a nation to shame even if they're watching multiple live productions of *Tallin's Got Talent*.

EXCUSES

Are innumerable. You will meet thousands of them in your career for those you work with will have one for *every* misdemeanour and *every* cock-up.

However, as I can list only a few of them here, I will mostly concentrate on excuses for non-appearance by the Half (see *Half*). Be assured that they are all true examples of a major art for they were told by people who utterly believed their own stories.

Public Transport has to be an odds-on favourite. I sometimes wonder if the Office of National Statistics is quite aware of the suicidal epidemic encountered nightly by the theatre profession on Underground and train services. I know the poor bloody drivers have a rough time of it, but surely most of our actors' minds must also be permanently scarred.

Other perennial favourites for being late for work or being just too late for it include:

"I left the stove on"
"I left the bath running"
"I have a gas leak"
"My boiler's blown up."
"My plumber's two hours late in coming"

Some are blatantly stupid:

"I locked myself out" (dumb)
"I've locked myself in" (dumber)

Better, are the more imaginative variety such as the double catastrophe: "My garden gate blew off in the wind and I can't lock my back door."

And:

"I've been hit on the head by a hub cap"
"I thought my waters broke"
"I'm still pissed from last night"
"My mum sat and squashed the life out of my @#&%! cat"
"I thought it was Sunday"
Slightly more life-threatening:

"I was driving in, on the Purley Way, when I got sucked into the slipstream of this funeral cortege. I was boxed in three behind the hearse for half an hour until I ended up at the crematorium. And you know where that is... Purley."

My own personal favourite for non-arrival is when I was phoned by two young actors to be told that unfortunately they couldn't come to work that evening, as they couldn't afford the fare.
Charitably, I sent a taxi to Battersea to bring them in to Victoria, and didn't dock them for the ride until their next week's payday.

EXIT

When you enter an auditorium, you will see this word on signs glowing feebly in the dark over several doors. Be assured that it is not an in-your-face advertisement for the Voluntary Euthanasia Society but a legal requirement of Health and Safety, a department which some deluded people indeed believe has hidden ties to the Voluntary Euthanasia Society.

EXPENSES

Are unavoidable. Clothes, haircuts, make-up, taxis, and that's just to get you to the interview. Once you've landed the job remember that every receipt counts, especially if it's someone else's.

FAIR

F IS FOR:

FAIR

If someone tells you that their show is doing 'fair' you'll know it's in foul trouble.

This again dates back to Shakspeer (see *Unmentionable, The*).

FAIRIES

"There are fairies at the bottom of my garden," sang Douglas Byng, who won't mean a thing, unless you're in your eighties, and, if you are, what are you doing up so late anyway and buying a book like this?

FALLING

Everyone falls over occasionally. It can be undignified in public so try not to do it too often or people may get the right impression. It should also only ever be done at deck level. It's really not wise to fall off a tallescope. The first twenty feet are fine – the last foot's fatal.

FALSE STAGE (a)

Do not be frightened of stepping onto a false stage. You will not disappear into a dark abyss and wake up in a deserted crew room. False stages are laid like so many other things theatrical because they are often in better shape than the real McCoy. If they're not, it's so that a revolve or automation tracks can be fitted and not leave huge holes in the theatre's stage when the day of the 'Get Out' comes around.

FANS

Are a cheap theatre's air conditioning.

FARCE

As we know it now, is a fast-paced style of comedy, sophisticated and often sexual.

It originated in France towards the end of the 19th century, written mostly by Georges Feydeau, whose plays are still produced in Paris to this day.

Over here, the sexual element was initially largely suppressed – witness the gentility of Pinero's plays and others such as *Charley's Aunt* – but these were succeeded and broadened by Ben Travers in the 1930s. This art form reached its pinnacle of popularity with the Whitehall Farces of the 1950s, 60s and 70s, many of which were written by that great master of the art, Ray Cooney.

Fashions change and nowadays farce has for the moment sadly lost the core of its popularity, though *One Man, Two Guv'nors* raises hope.

The word is wrongly used as a derogative to describe ludicrous failures rather than the art of masterful comic timing and inventiveness, and Oh! Whoops! There go my trousers!

FART

Encountered but not encouraged in the workplace. If your gases are persistent perhaps it is time to take a professional stance and reap the rewards. May I recommend the career of Joseph Pujol? In the 1890s the box office receipts for Sarah Bernhardt were 8000 francs per performance but Monsieur Pujol, aka *Le Petomane*, took 20,000 on a single Sunday show at *Le Moulin Rouge*. Joseph would literally sing through his arse and, when the songs had run their course, could, if his wind was in the right direction, blow out the gas foot lights. A hard act to follow.

FASHION

Usually comes round in this business. Never throw away those clothes you wore in the last century. Just wear them in a retro way.

FEAR

Everyone's frightened in this business. It's the great leveller and gives theatre its impetus. So if someone asks why you're shaking like a jellyfish you've now got another reason.

FEATRE

The egcepted dyslexic way of spelling out watt business you're in. You may never thinish your sentince but many of your fallow wurkers will emphasise with ewe.

FELLATIO

Is NOT a Verdi Opera.

FINALE (the)

Is usually very sensibly placed at the end of a musical, and is the final scene before the curtain call.

FIRE

Has closed more shows and theatres over the years than any other disaster.

Shakepurrs's Globe set the fashion on 29 June 1613 during a performance of *All is True* when sparks from a stage-cannon salute ignited the thatched roof. The whole building was consumed but "only one man had his breeches set on fire that would perhaps have broiled him if he had not, by the benefit of a provident wit, put it out with bottle ale".

Since then there have been hundreds of conflagrations all over the world and unfortunately some audiences have been less fortunate than those of *All is True* (see *Mister Jet*).

FIREARMS

Are comforting when travelling late at night on the Underground. You'll need a licence, though, to use one in a theatre.

FIREMEN

Are much admired by certain members of the profession. That is one of the reasons you will find them lurking in the wings – the admirers that is, for the firemen are usually out front during a performance. They come into their own, as it were, well after the show when they gather up huge bunches of chains and padlocks and rattle off into the night to secure every possible entrance. But by then, it must be said, most of their admirers have made an inevitably sad and lonely exit.

FIRST AID

First Aid is for First Aiders. I state this because you must always let the professionals have first crack.

No matter how much you may want to give the kiss of life, remember there are qualified people hanging about all parts of the theatre who have a diploma in an art so often administered in the dark of an auditorium.

FIRST NIGHT PARTIES

Are usually held AFTER a First Night, except when a show's so bad and the atmosphere so tense that the producers decide to have a party the night before to make sure some people will attend.

Parties come in all shapes and sizes, as do the guests. Musicals tend to have larger First Night Parties than straight plays which means that there will be less to eat.

FIRST NIGHTS

Are not those spent with whom you fancy but the official opening nights of a show. This is when the critics are invited by the producers to review the production.

Note that they are invited. This means that they have to be given a pair of seats as well as two programmes plus an optional free drink and anything else they may require to aid their enjoyment (see *Booster Cushions*). Please note that the critics always sit separate from each other in aisle seats and always in the Stalls. That is one reason casts always play to the Stalls and never lift their heads to the Dress Circle, unless it's falling down.

FIRST WORDS

An Actor's are always: "How big's my part?" But an Audience's are: "How long does it last?"

FISH

The old rule still applies that fish should not be consumed in the theatre. This goes back to the bad old days of fierce competition between starving casts and theatre cats on Saturday nights and the dangers of flying batter.

Even now that cats have been banished it is still advisable to only smuggle in raw fish, for the fragrant aroma of the chippie will always stick to your clothes or someone else's.

FIVE (the)

Nothing to do with Enid Blyton's famous quintet but the backstage call to let all know that they are ten minutes away from curtain up.

FLASH BOX (a)

Must be treated with respect and handled with care. It is a robust metal container in which pyrotechnics are set and ignited by means of an electrical charge. If you need one and want to be perceived as technically up for it, ask for a pyropad at Le Maître.

FLATS

Are, in the theatrical sense, upright pieces of scenery constructed of wooden skeletal frames covered in canvas, in various sizes, but all flat.

FLIES

Are found in most theatres. Try to keep them away from the actors as they spread diseases (flies) and have been known to nest in wigs (actors).

FLOAT (1)

You do this to a flat, when you let it fall gently from its upright position flat onto its face on the deck. This is by design not accident, so to avoid one, make sure that no actor is standing in its flight path. It won't in general harm the actor, but the flat will bear an impression of his face for some time and upset those of a sensitive nature.

FLOAT (2)

Stage management often ask if they can float. This is not a desire to return to the womb or a tentative first step towards walking on water.

A float is a complex technical term for being absent from work in the comforting knowledge that your duties will be covered by someone else. That is, of course, if that someone else has been informed or booked (see *Nightly Check List*).

FLOPS

Are never flops; they are short runs.

FLUFF (to)

Offstage, actors have been known to fluff pompoms, pooches and pillows but on stage, when faced with long runs and short memories, it's strictly their lines they'll fluff. It's a different world in the cinema.

FLYS (the)

Is another of those theatrical danger areas and you must be strict and very firm with any of the cast who break the 'No Entry' rule.

The flys are nearly always worked from a gallery positioned high up above the stage, jutting out from the side wall. This is where the art of flying scenery is performed using individual lines and counterweight systems, and it is the home of the flymen, skilled artists of their craft.

Woe betide anyone who enters their domain uninvited or unannounced. I say this because those of a sensitive nature could be shocked by the nakedness of some of the occupants, either pinned to the walls or clamped to the cradles. I think, all in all, that it can be truly said that the flys is one of the hottest spots in theatre.

FOH

Stands for Front of House, meaning anywhere in the area of a theatre on the audience side of the proscenium arch.

FOOT (to)

Not a command as "To Horse" as can happen when Hotspur forgets the rest of his speech in the Histories, but in one meaning a simple request from one honest mechanic to another should he (or you) be obliged to climb a dodgy ladder resting against a shaky set.

By putting your best foot forward and on to the first decrepit rung, you are protecting his teeth and other remaining parts of his body from grievous harm.

To foot a flat is another theatrical skill for your lower extremities. Place your left or right boot on the bottom end of a prostrate flat. Stand dead still and calmly watch as your colleagues at each side of the other end lift and elevate the flat to its working upright position. Remove your boot. You have now footed a flat.

FOOTLIGHTS

Long gone are the days when theatres needed footlights. These were rows of lights, originally candles; then lamps, powered first by gas and then electricity permanently placed on the front aprons of stages. They helped banish the shadows from below actors' faces and this naked exposure in turn caused the end of the tradition of multiple double chins in the theatrical profession. This age of the perfect profile lasted until the development of powerful modern spots which saw the demise of the footlight and the return of the double chin, albeit now mostly single in this health-conscious age.

FORESTAGE (the)

Is the stage area in proscenium theatres in front of the iron and the house curtain.

It has, like the foreskin, been considerably circumcised since its conception. No longer can the cast strut their stuff in revivals of Elizabethan or Restoration drama right under the noses and within touching distance of their audiences. This does have some advantage though in the avoidance of bad odours and disease.

FOUR WALLS DEAL (a)

Means that a producer's hire of a theatre does not include the permanent staff such as the box office, the electrics or stage staff. This practice is more usually found in the United States than in the UK.

FOURTH WALL (the)

Does not refer to a great grandson of Max but to that invisible wall which covers every proscenium arch and through which every audience can see.

FRENCH FLAT

A folding flat that, when opened fully and battened out, can be used as the back piece of a box set. It can also be flown and dropped when needed and if all this sounds slightly seedy and Francophobic, it isn't.

FRENCHMAN (a)

If you ever have the urge to hang one, or at least are told to, is a flown flat comprised of a combination of a number of flats bolted together.

FRENCH NAILS

Are, however, seldom worn by those who handle French flats.

FRIDGES

All modern theatres now have fridges and some of them even work.
Try and make sure yours does before the cast get into the theatre, and once you are happy with its performance get a lock put on it before you stock it up. That way your petty cash is safe and the Petit Chablis chilled.

FRONT CLOTH

A front cloth is often used instead of house tabs. This could be because the latter have gone missing or are on loan or because the design of the show requires a visible statement for the audience to see before curtain up. This will on some shows lull them into a state of total false security.

FULL UP

When the lights on stage during a show go to 'full up' they are at their brightest intensity. This means that it's time for either an in-your-face musical number or the leading actor is making his entrance. On the other hand the board operator may have pushed the wrong button.

FUNAMBULIST

Not someone who loiters round your local undertaker but a rope or wire walker.

This is a skill you won't have to learn yourself unless you have to deliver a final written warning to one of the cast in *Barnum!* or *Cirque du Soleil.*

GAFFER TAPE

G IS FOR:

GAFFER TAPE

As used originally by film gaffers, is a wad of sticky black tape, absolutely essential for anyone, even of the least technical ability, who is working backstage in the theatre.

It can hold broken window glass together, keep car doors secured and patch many a hole on walls, floors, shoes, roofs and trousers.

GAITER (a)

Is worn, one on each leg, by bishops in farces.

GARDEN (the)

Is the familiar term for the Royal Opera House, Covent Garden; used even by those who can't afford a seat.

GARRICK (David)

Was the first actor to be deemed 'respectable'. Garrick managed to make the audience listen to him for a full performance. This feat meant a stop to the time-honoured tradition of the throwing of rotten fruit every night at the cast.

Even so, his management of Drury Lane Theatre saw some spectacular riots, the best being in 1755 when he brought over from Paris an elaborate ballet titled *The Chinese Festival*.

It proved to be not the best-timed decision of his career, as war was just about to be declared between France and England. The ballet opened on 12 November to "a good deal of hissing... noise, tumult and commotion" in the King's presence. "His majesty was amazed at the uproar, but, being told that it was because people hated the French, he smiled and withdrew from a scene of confusion."

Garrick, having invested some £2000 in bringing these froggy dancers over, was loath to cut his losses. He kept the ballet on, but tensions soon reached fever pitch between the different social classes in the audience.

On the evening of the 18th the house waited for three tense hours for the show to start while the orchestra, bloody-minded as ever, serenaded them with patriotic songs such as *The Roast Beef of Old England.* Predictably at curtain up it was on with both the motley and the riot.

The Drury Lane prompter Richard Cross recorded that, "...the rout went on. The boxes drove many out of the pit and broken heads were plenty on both sides. The dance, began, was stopped and so, again and again. While this was doing, numbers were assembled in the passages of the pit, broke down and were getting into the cellar, but were repulsed by our scenemen etc. Heavy blows on both sides."

Special Constables and the Army were called out by Justice Henry Fielding in time to prevent a section of the mob completely destroying Garrick's nearby house but the rioters still in the theatre "...tore up the benches and threw them into the pit on the opposing party; they broke all the mirrors, the chandeliers etc and tried to massacre everybody."

It was then, though, I am proud to relate, that an early CSM obviously must have taken control. "But as there is a magnificent organisation in this theatre, in three minutes all the décor had been removed, all the traps were ready to come into play to swallow up those who might venture up, all the wings were filled with men armed with sticks, swords, halberds etc and behind the scenes the great reservoir was ready to be opened to drown those who might fall on the stage itself."

So, the next time Miss 'Silly' Tilly Tremble is late on with a broken fingernail and ends up with a slow clap, remind her quietly of 1755.

GAS

Is not used in theatres these days. So, if a depressed actor says before the show that he's going to gas himself, please remember it's an empty threat until he gets home.

GAUZE CLOTH (a)

Made from fine netting, is, when lit from the front, a solid cloth. It becomes transparent, however, when the first LX state (see *LX*) is lowered and lights are brought up on stage behind it. This effect is often used by designers as a delightful form of reveal which can become slightly less delightful if the actors are not in position or in positions not of a becoming nature.

GBS

Not to be confused with GBH, these initials stand for George Bernard Shaw who at one time challenged the supremacy of Shakespeer as our premier dramatist though not, of course, at the same time.

GEL

Has a dual identity in theatre. There's the sticky, gooey stuff that wig mistresses ladle out to actors to calm disobedient locks and fly-away curls. Then there's the fine, thin sheet of transparent tinted plastic that makes actors, wigs, and even their mistresses alluring when it is positioned in front of a lamp to colour its beam.

GENESIUS

Is the patron Saint of Actors. A Roman thespian, his last performance in AD 303 was before the Emperor Diocletian. In a pro-pagan parody mocking Christian baptism, Genesius, to the horror of his prompter, went off script, declared that he could see angels and demanded to be baptised on stage. The Emperor in turn demanded his execution and he was duly beheaded. His feast day is on 25 August and he is still widely venerated throughout the Catholic world.

GET IN (a)

Is not only an admonition from a grumpy cab driver. It's that glorious moment for a stage manager when, as the sun rises, the 'nuts and bolts' of his trade – the set – arrives outside the theatre in its pantechnicon.

Then, with care and dedication, it is carefully off-loaded by the crew to be put together in its entirety for the very first time. All its components, once safely in, are laid delicately down or to the side until their moment comes to be erected. Then skilful hands will gently raise them up while others, with minute accuracy, drill holes, fix pins, screw and smoothly attach each piece to its fellows.

It is a wonderful sight to watch, especially if it's arrived at the right theatre.

GET OUT (a)

Happens on a rainy night. The tired old set's prised apart with crowbars and hammers. And to a chorus of cursing, thrown on to the truck and off to the dump.

GHERKINS

Not Joanna Lumley's plucky little soldiers with their wicked sharp knives but a large, small or medium-sized pickled cucumber you may come across at cheaper First Night Parties.

If you are still confused, just eat the latter.

GHOST WALKS (the)

Are not those that take you on an exhausting tour of the shabbier parts of Victorian London while being constantly harangued by some all-knowing, opinionated and monotonous bore. That's an experience you can have anyway at any theatre that's mounting a Dickens adaptation.

No, the ghost walks refers to the CSMs, who, on Thursday nights, glide through the dressing rooms, distributing the cast's wage slips as fast as they can. This gives the actors no time to open them and ask awkward questions.

The expression derives from Sheakspier again and refers to Hamlet's father, most foully poysoned til deade and hence a ghost. But, you may well ask, why does he walk rather than float? And for that matter what has that got to do with a CSM?

So let me set your mind, if not my spelling, finally to rest. In days gone by, CSMs, despite all their other diverse duties, would also be made to play the Ghost. Hence, verily or at least sometimes they would walk around between cues doling out the groat or half-sovereign wage owed to each actor. So thank you and godnyhte.

GHOSTS

ALL theatres are haunted. Take my word for it but, if you still don't, go buy my forthcoming book, the aptly titled *All Theatres are Haunted*.

GHOULS/NOSFERATU

I do not wish to disturb you unduly, especially if you are of a nervous disposition, but I think it only fair to let you into a closely shrouded secret unknown to most. Some theatres are increasingly becoming the domain of branches of the Undead.

It started years ago. Shows that should have long been buried spawned them and enticed them out of their foul lairs into ours and now they are amongst us.

Nightly they appear. The most basic float outside stage doors making gurgling, squealing sounds as hapless turns turn out. Flee before they start to follow you home.

Some of them crouch in dimly lit Upper Circles and claim to be mere ushers. Never be deceived. A blank stare at the mention of Edgar Allan Poe is a dead giveaway.

The worst and cunning few are already in our midst. Eternally, suspiciously young, they will be so grateful for "a word of advice" – until you start to give it. Should you do so, you are doomed. Hours of torture will ensue as they bore you to death with tales of a thousand performances watched, before their thirteen failed open auditions and then the casting director's final, fatal mistake.

Be prepared. Don't let them start. Tell them to never, ever eat garlic again before a show, and that comes from the lips of *Nosferatu*.

GIN

London Gin has been the mainstay of theatre audiences since the 18th century. Only Beefeater is still distilled on a large scale in our capital these days but theatre bars still count the tipple as their best seller even if it sounds if it's come all the way from Bombay, and, at around £10.80 for a double these days (without tonic) it bloody well should.

GLAMOUR

Glamour in the theatre ends at the pass door.

GNASH

To gnash properly please remember that though the word has a silent 'g', the action doesn't so be sure to have a dentist in attendance.

GO ON (to)

When an actor goes on, it not only means he's talking about his performance but also that he's walked on stage even if he's forgotten that there's an audience out there and he's still talking about his performance.

GO ON COLD (to)

Means when an actor makes an appearance without any rehearsal in a valiant attempt to keep the curtain up. This does happen at times and, though very scary for the player, is even more frightening for the rest of the cast.

GO ON FOR (to)

However, when you hear that he is going on for another actor it means that he is an understudy and is going to play the other's part, owing to the other's absence or illness.

GO UP (to)

Is the American expression for 'to dry'. To 'Go Down' is not.

GOBOS

The word itself stands for Graphic Optical Black Outs. Many theatre folk often have gobos of their own, but as far as a show's Electrics Department are concerned their gobos, which are placed in front of lamps, are made of metal or glass with areas that light cannot penetrate. This means that all manner of patterns – clouds, shadows et cetera – can be projected onto a set or cloth.

GODS (the)

Few of us see the Gods these days. Theatre Galleries are just too far up to make it there before curtain down. That's, of course, if they're actually open and not condemned. Woodworm and dry rot are rife and both ruin an audience's clothes and make-up.

GOD MIC (the)

Is often heard but seldom seen unless caught in mid flight in the general direction of a hapless, out-of-step ensemble. It is a blunt instrument of terror and used most effectively in dark auditoriums by directors or choreographers too shy or ugly to be viewed in daylight. God mics are battery-operated these days so when you are sick of verbal violence, sabotage is possible.

GOFER (a)

Not to be confused with a gobo, a gofer is really a film term for a runner. Runners are sometimes used during play rehearsal periods but not that often as they expect at least to get their travelling expenses. Many in the theatre prefer to use young people who have requested work experience, a term interpreted literally by managements. They work for the experience.

GOITRE (a)

Not to be confused with a Gaiter, this is an ongoing medical condition and not something stuck in the throat. You don't see so many actors these days with goitres but, even if you do, do not attempt First Aid.

GRAND GUIGNOL (Le)

Not the French acting equivalent of the Great Gambon but French nonetheless.

Again, like most French theatre, it was in vogue at the turn of the last century and was a name given to short violent plays where throats were cut, blood spurted and audiences fainted. Due for a revival soon, one can only hope.

GRATUITIES

Is the smart word for tips. My best tip is to; because of all the obvious benefits it will bring.

Your mail will be hand-delivered, your office fumigated and your name remembered, so very handy if you are having a senior moment.

GREEN ROOM (the)

Is basically a room backstage in common use by all the company purely for the social necessities of a nice cup of tea and a good old bitch.

"But," you are asking, "Why does it have to be green?"

The short answer is, of course, that it doesn't. It could be red, white or blue as far as the paint's concerned. Only the name is traditional, the first written reference being in a play in 1678.

In 1701 Colley Cibber, the actor and dramatist, was more and quite explicit, "I do know London pretty well, and the Side Box, Sir, and behind the scenes; ay, and the Green Room, and all the Girls and Women Actresses there."

This could imply that its original use was as a backstage knocking shop, but we must remember that actresses of that era made more money at it out of the theatre than in it and so it probably really was a room for real rest rather than restful wrestling.

There is the theory that green is a soothing colour, but if the room at Drury Lane was actually green in 1735, it did not prevent an argument over a wig. This culminated in the actor Charles Macklin killing his fellow player Thomas Hallam by a sharp thrust of his cane, through said fellow's left eye and onwards into the brain.

Macklin mounted his own defence and lived to be one hundred and ten for he was acquitted, of course, to a round of applause.

Lastly, another theory is that it is linked by its proximity to the old French theatre expression for the stage itself Le Vert, meaning The Green. However, these days, should any old performer tell you that he'll meet you on the The Green, he probably means Turnham.

GREMLINS

Is not just a film. It is a recognised fact that these creatures delight in infesting the computers that program and drive large automated sets and so make these marvels of engineering stop in mid track or flight.

It is also a little known fact that the worst of them have been known, and on one occasion seen, to enter the bodies of certain automation operators. How else can one account for their behaviour?

GRID

Grids are found high above most theatre stages. Directly underneath the roof, a varied number of steel girders span the width of the building from wall to wall. These are closely laid together and collectively become the grid. It is from these that all the various pulleys, joists and rigging for flying are attached and I seriously warn those CSMs who suffer from vertigo not to venture there nor, for that matter, short-sighted CSMs, for there are gaps between the girders waiting to be filled, however briefly. Some theatres have a flashing warning light by the side of the stage which, when lit, indicates that there is 'Grid Work in Progress' and that Safety Helmets should be worn. It has always struck me that one of those falling from the grid could do as much harm as a spanner but then I'm no H & S expert.

GRIEF COUNSELLING

Is not only a tad depressing but very time-consuming as the theatre attracts a desperately unfair proportion of clinically sad people. Mourning may become Electra but I'm hard put to think of anyone else whom it fits like a glove, discounting professional pallbearers and crematorium caretakers. If you do have this professional qualification and have a compulsion to practise, stick to one-legged contortionists. They are few and far between for reasons of health and safety and once your desire is slated you can tell them truthfully and without sarcasm to "hop off".

GROINS

Should never be disturbed. They are absolutely vital to the sea defences of the eastern and southern shores of England.

GROMMETS

When you're having problems with your inner self (see *Doubt*) this may also be because you are having difficulties with your inner ear which may have silently filled up with fluid. This can happen to younger ASMs and is commonly called 'Glue Ear'. It's easily treatable and all you have to do is have a grommet inserted, but please take note of the spelling if you are one of those self-medicators. A grummet should always be avoided (see *Grummet*).

GROSS (the)

Is what the value of the house is before any deductions are made from it for such things as VAT and commissions. Always remember to give your producer the net figure should he phone, so as to avoid eventual disappointment and foul language directed at you rather than the fickle public.

GROUCHO (the)

Is a club in Dean Street, Soho, and very sensibly bars the use of mobile phones. Always tell everybody you're a member even if you are not. That way, once you're supposedly in there, 'being there' is the perfect excuse why you missed all those trying to get hold of you with their own excuses.

GROUND PLAN

Ground plans are the Designer's scaled plans of the set. It is rather essential that they are accurate and also that they are accurately read. Failure to do so by the Designer in the first instance, can lead to the second act of a play living on a truck outside the dock doors for Act One.

An error by stage management in the second instance can also mean that when the cast manage to squeeze themselves on stage they find that the ballroom scene is suitable only for solo dancers.

GROUND ROW (a)

Is a low piece of scenery, usually placed so as to hide lights or small actors.

GROUNDLINGS (the)

Is the name for those spectators who stood to watch Shackspeer's works rather than pay the extra groat for a bench seat. They are mentioned in Hamlet's speech to the players and this tradition together with the name has now been revived since the opening of the Globe at Southwark.

GROUP BOOKINGS

Are very important for the longevity of musicals. They are what used to be called 'party bookings' and comprise any number of people who collectively have been sold tickets to see the same show and travel to see it all together on the same coach. Whether it is actually the show they want to see is, of course, another matter and whether they arrive at the theatre in time to see it is in God's hands, or whoever else is holding the steering wheel of the coach.

GRUMMET (a)

A very useful piece of static metal rather than a misspelt peace of animated plasticine (Gromit), a grummet is used to secure a throw line or sash to a flat or piece of scenery.

HABERDASHERY

H IS FOR:

HABERDASHERY

Now here's a word that may well confuse a new stage manager.

He or she, more likely than not, will never have come across someone in the act of haberdashering.

That is because these days, the outlets for such trade are few and far between. However, Wardrobe Mistresses and Masters of 'uncertain age' persist in disguising their purchases of elasticated rubbered garments under that heading in their petty cash.

HAIR

If someone refers to *Hair* they are either talking about the definitive Sixties musical or someone else's barnet. Or again they may just be exercising their accents as in 'hair today and gawn tomorrow'.

HALF (the)

Stands for half an hour. It's not a correct measurement of time for in British Theatre the Half is thirty-five minutes long. That's in contrast to the American Theatre where the Half is exactly thirty minutes even though that doesn't make their productions any more accurate.

The Half is that special time when the cast 'prepare' for their performance. No actor follows the same routine. A few go through their lines, some warm up their voices, many reapply their make-up, and most are on their laptops checking Facebook. That's if they're actually in the building by the Half (see *Excuses*).

As the minutes tick by the tension palpably mounts for soon it will be the Quarter, then the Five and then Beginners. It is then that you hear, from behind closed dressing-room doors, groans of anguish as crosswords are abandoned, and foul language as costumes are struggled into and abused. As everything is five minutes early they've still got time to realise they're in the wrong costume or dressing room, change again and make it to the stage for curtain up.

So why is it five minutes too long? The answer lies in the past, as so much else does in this business.

Before tannoys were invented, each theatre had to employ at least one Call Boy.

This lad or, more often, old lag, would wait by the prompt corner and when the stage manager announced that it was time for the Half, would set off around the dressing rooms to echo this call. Even if he had only one good leg, it was reckoned that the whole round trip should take no more than five minutes before he got back to base, and by then, of course, it would be exactly the Half.

HALITOSIS

Is best left at home.

HAM

Is a derogatory expression often used by an actor to describe another's performance and one that indicates a coarse, flamboyant, over-the-top interpretation of the part.

This opinion is often vocalised when the recipient of this insult receives bigger laughs, applause and reviews.

HAMLET

Is a witty cartoon pig in *The Stage*. Not to be confused with the Prince of Denmark, which is, of course, a pub in South London.

HAND (do you need a?)

If you should come across an old trouper trying to mount a tread or turn the pages of his script, never ask if he needs a hand. He will always reply with: "No applause, please" and promptly fall over.

HEADLINE ACT (a)

Means whoever, or whatever (in the case of Susie, The Singing Seal) is topping the evening's bill.

HEADS!

Is a precautionary word of warning shouted backstage. If you hear it, look upwards and, if necessary, move to safety for something potentially nasty such as a claw hammer could be falling from the grid, or a heavy piece of scenery may be flying in.

HEALTH AND SAFETY

Is taken very seriously these days. So seriously in fact, that it can be quite crippling to this business. Its regulations come in massive tomes and in order to avoid severe accidents these should never be dropped on peoples' heads or toes.

HEALTH WARNINGS

Should always be prominently displayed and those of you of a nervous disposition will be comforted to know that they are. I read the following Health Warning only the other day in an Investment letter:

"The content of this promotion has not been approved by an authorised person within the meaning of the Financial Services and Markets Act 2000. Reliance on this promotion for the purpose of engaging in any investment activity may expose an individual to a significant risk of losing all of the property or other assets invested."

Stern stuff eh? And probably why these days those more nervous theatre investors bet on horses rather than on the next possible *Cats*.

HEDDA

If an actor tells you he's doing Hedda he's referring to the Ibsen play *Hedda Gabler* even if he is also sleeping with the leading lady.

HEMP HOUSE (a)

Is perfectly legal in our dramatic world. It refers to the odd theatre that has so far resisted the advances of modern flying technology and so obliges visiting managements to engage an army of flymen to fly their scenery.

HENRYS (going to do the)

A phrase used by actors to indicate that they are employed and Stratford-bound, usually by Avon as East doesn't usually have the budget to mount more than one Henry at a time.

HERNIA

A useful ailment to allude to should you be asked to carry anything heavier than an envelope.

HEROES

Theatre has always had its heroes and relies heavily on their legends, dead or alive, to help glamorise and sustain a pretty ramshackle profession. Please be kind about and to them. Heroes also have feet of clay, even if they're clad in Jimmy Choos.

HISS

And boo are sounds which you don't often hear these days, audiences being far more forgiving than of yore. However, they are not totally redundant and can still be encountered occasionally in Italian Opera Houses when good taste prevails over bad performances, especially when they've cost more than the original Puccini score.

HISTORIES (the)

Are not a television series like *The Sopranos*. They are in fact the Bard's collection of History plays – *Richard II*; *Henry IV parts 1 and 2*; *Henry V*; *Henry VI parts 1, 2 and 3* and finally *Richard III* – and deal with statesmanship and honour, plus lashings of pride, lust, greed and gratuitous violence.

Great fun. Grab a production.

HISTRIONIC

If a member of your cast is having a histrionic it has nothing to do with the preceding subject or a strong spirit from Mexico. They are merely overwrought, emotional and, in other words, as normal as they can be.

HOD

Stands for Head of Department. You will find Heads of Department scattered over every part of the theatre, but when they're on their feet they are the titular bosses of wigs or wardrobe, stage or electrics, sound or automation, box office or catering, to name but eight. Many answer to none save the Theatre Manager not only because some are hard-of-hearing misanthropes, but because they also have to get signatures of approval on time sheets and order forms.

Departments, as do their heads, vary widely in size according to the individual theatre or production. They can be huge, with deputies and myriad assistants in the chain of command, or literally departments of one. These solitary individuals can sometimes be glimpsed at dawn or dusk in dusty corridors or darkened auditoriums. Please remember to respect the privacy and dignity of the housekeeper or company manager, even if you can't remember their names.

HOSIERY

Another antique word scribbled by the Wardrobe department as an explanation for receipts that simply state "£10.00". Some zealous Company Managers do investigate further before reimbursing this otherwise bald bit of paper. However this can lead to very embarrassing scenes and undesired knowledge. After all, antique actors have enough problems working through prickly heat and dhobie itch. I cannot name one who would wish to parade their collection of carbuncles, corns and calluses naked on stage when their antique atheletes' feet can be hidden by antique hosiery.

HOOK (the)

Is not a reference to that sea-tossed part of Holland where the Van Hook Familie Theater company ply their spumy trade upon the Pier, but a British theatre word oozing with its very own nautical connection.

The Hook is indeed an actual boat hook and one used very occasionally to get high actors or low comedians off stage when all other methods have failed. "Hook him, Mr Christian" bawled from the wings, never fails dramatically nor really diminishes the Importance of Being Earnest.

HOUSE (the)

Is another name for your audience or auditorium and not to be confused with *House Beautiful*, the title of a Broadway show immortalised by Dorothy Parker's pithy review "*House Beautiful* is play lousy."

HOUSE TO HALF

Is a phrase similar in dramatic intensity to one of those expressions used by Jack Hawkins out and up there on the bridge in *The Cruel Sea*.

It's traditionally said with great calmness by the DSM as all the backstage elements that make up a show – the actors, the crew, even some say, the scenery – prepare for that serene moment that is Curtain Up.

Front of House, of course, is a different story. As the auditorium lights fade to fifty percent, ushers scurry away dropping their programmes and those annoying voices and the bewildered audience left in the aisles, or sitting in the wrong seats, grapple or grope with each other in the sudden gloaming. "Carry On Theatre."

HUBRIS

Is ever present in our business.

HUMAN ALPHABET (the)

This novelty act never really took off. The three-man team could indeed become every letter of the alphabet with great ingenuity.

However, they missed their one chance of stardom when asked by the theatre manager to busk it for once and spell out the immortal message "Ladies and Gentlemen your attention please! Mafeking is relieved!!"

Nerves got the better of them, and they wrong-footed with 'Manchester', 'Mansfield' and 'Macclesfield' before hitting the right dorp.

By the time they'd spelt out the full sentence, half the audience were asleep and the other half had drifted off to the pub. Their decline was fast. Inevitably they ended up bottom of the bill at Los Burlesquos, Barcelona, opening and closing the show with a single, sad "Ola".

HYENA

A journalist of the lesser variety, living off salacious stories about the celebrities of the theatre which are usually hand fed to them by non-celebrities of the theatre.

HYPERVENTILATION

Is self-induced. Not advisable for your position of authority, but should you come across a member of your cast or audience suffering from it and feel obliged to render assistance, you must make use of an empty brown paper bag. Remember, this is for them to breathe into and not to be sick into. The state of today's budgets dictate that it should be reusable.

HYSTERIA

Again you will probably have to deal with this common theatrical common problem.

A gentle manner, a soft voice and the same paper bag are required.

If the first two remedies don't calm, give up on them, turn away, turn back, slip the paper bag over the hysteric's head and give them a good, hard slapping.

That may help and if not, they won't know who did it and you can move on to deal with the next crisis.

IAGO

I IS FOR:

IAGO

One of the greatest enigmatic villains of all time, Iago destroys Othello, but why?

His behaviour is uncannily like some of today's theatre critics.

IBS

One moment you are in fine flow, the next you are strutting and fretting all over the stage for seeming hours, verse and worse pouring out all over your fellow players. Be calm, be still, behave, you have what any company manager worth his salt can diagnose in one: Irritable Bard Syndrome. Luckily this malady is not deadly and will only occur towards the end of one of those interminable Festivals where the whole canon is attempted, most frequently in rural Warwickshire, Ontario and downtown Southwark.

However, if you feel this minor ailment is beneath you, then go for broke, avoid such an engagement and seek out a placement at an Agatha Christie Season. When that major ICS inevitably comes, you will have a splendid choice of weapon – knife, poison or revolver – to wreak total havoc on all those actors who have suspected or accused you of ruining their denouements.

ICE CREAM

Is a diminishing audience treat these days as an average family of four can scarcely afford one pot between them. This leads to frequent nasty scenes of a domestic nature in the interval. However, if you're working FOH, never intervene, as your uniform will identify you as an unacceptable face of capitalism, and you'll be rounded on and have one of those tiny plastic spoons stuck right up your nose.

It is also advisable not to loiter directly underneath the front of the Dress Circle during public and school holidays. Hair can suffer terrible damage when a combination of animal grease and vegetable colourings unite with chemical dyes.

ICONS

The theatre is awash with icons but it is very important that you choose the right ones to support, champion and finally put down. To judge someone's performance, it is perhaps best to have seen it and this, with the present cost of theatre tickets, puts one at a constant disadvantage.

A quickly sketched opinion can be formed from a glance at the papers or from listening to tourists on the Tube but neither are totally reliable.

Therefore to avoid ridicule when asked for your opinion, stick to dead icons and the deader the better. Who can argue your claim that Edmund Shakespeare was a better actor than his brother, or deny Fanny Kemble's chief attraction?

IGNORANCE

"Where ignorance is bliss, 'Tis folly to be wise." So wrote Thomas Gray and it's a good quote to remember when you're asked such stock questions as: "Do you think I'll be offered the part?" or "Are we going to run till Christmas?"

ILLNESS

Is rather common in some companies. Casts come down with a variety of ailments headed by that special favourite, one-day flu. Their chests and throats are also very vulnerable and their chances of avoiding food poisoning almost minimal. Add Deng Fever, the Black Death and Yellow Tongue and you would naturally think that this potentially show-stopping Passchendaele of Diseases would depress even the most hardened CSM.

Never! Because, you'll be glad to know, these combined epidemics, despite all their vileness, curiously only lay an actor low for twenty-four days. After that he's suddenly up and running with the best of them and fully deserving a consistent, and unvaried wage packet.

IMPROVISE

Please take care when asked to improvise. It can mean that the creators of your production have run out of script or ideas and you should not open yourself to criticism by volunteering to attempt a clever bit of business. That is, unless your claim to be a past member of Le Cirque Imaginaire proves not so much a figment as a concrete fact.

INCOMPETENCE

Is a charge that will no doubt be levelled at you from time to time. You must rise above it and carry on muddling through.

INCONTINENCE

Can strike at anytime to anybody anywhere. Be sure to have your briefcase always close at hand.

INITIATIVE

You would expect that initiative would be rewarded in this inspirational business.

However, please remember that, like those three old favourites of Prince Charles, it comes in degrees. You may indeed be thanked for bringing a stream of unasked-for skinny soya lattes to the bleary-eyed director at the start of a busy day's rehearsal and again a large Bloody Mary will go down well at lunchtime, but you certainly won't be appreciated when you present her with the bill at close of play. Know your place, love, and get real. So, if you have to use your initiative, use someone else's.

INSANITY

In this day and age does insanity really exist amongst our ranks? Or does it go hand in glove with the concept of our profession?

You will be deemed insane by friends and family when, having read this book, you first express a desire to enter the business. But not after you get your first job.

Some of the greatest theatrical roles such as King Lear and Caligula cover different aspects of insanity, but none of their portrayers are known to have been sectioned under the Mental Health Act.

Insanely optimistic productions are mounted continually by perfectly sane and sober producers. These manic follies are dismissed rather as commercial misjudgements.

The actor Richard Archer Prince, the murderer of fellow thespian William Terriss was found guilty and sent as a criminal lunatic to Broadmoor, but that was in 1898. Poor Dan Leno was in Camberwell House Asylum for several months, but that again was in 1903.

But today, are any of our contemporary actors mad? I am glad to answer with an emphatic 'No'. The advances in modern medical science, aka 'pills', means that we can judge them safely, even closely, at their face value. They can be seen to be what they are, merely ever so slightly eccentric, even if they do pull the wings off flats and flys.

INSPIRE

A very popular word and one well thought of in the profession.

It is much used by directors but is commonly confused by their captive audiences (meaning yourself) and the cast, with the similar-sounding 'expire' and 'perspire.'

To clear up this confusion please note that:

Some Directors seldom inspire.
Most Actors do often perspire.
All of us mortals have to expire.

INSURANCE

Just as wise producers take out a policy for a show, so should wise Stage Managers insure themselves.

Hair and teeth can fall out at any time and fallen arches can occur the very first time you cross the stage.

INTERESTING

The best retrospective word to describe a performance or play which has left you speechless.

INTERMISSION (the)

Is what happens in cinemas. The word should never to be used in theatrical parlance.

INTERVAL

Intervals are absolutely essential in this business and if some authors beg to differ, let them. Without an interval, a cast's collective bladder could explode and as most shows' audiences outnumber the casts, imagine the situation out front.

There are also bar profits to be considered. A sensible management always has the heating on high in the summer to ensure a demand for cold wines, beers and lagers, and if those run out, there's the comfort of the certainty of an even higher return on bottled water and ice creams.

IRON (the)

Not to be confused with that fine actor Jeremy, who is, of course, plural.

The Iron is a theatre's Fire Curtain which resides for most of a show above the proscenium opening. It straddles the whole and when lowered completely blocks out an audience or performance. This can be very useful on more riotous productions.

Irons do have a tendency to creep in so it's advisable to keep your actors and yourself always upstage of them.

IRONIC

And 'metaphor' have predictably been voted for the thirteenth year running as the two most predictable words to be used by a director in rehearsal.

I think it most important to point this out: It is surely high time that directors were made aware that most of their casts haven't a clue what these two vital words mean.

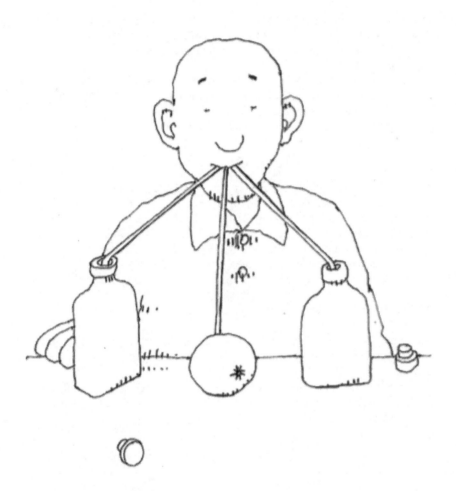

JAFFA

J IS FOR:

JAFFA

Jaffa Oranges are a fine tonic for a rundown actor when injected with gin or vodka.

JERK
(See *Knee*)

JEST

"Jest a joke" is a fitting retort to a boring story told by a boring person. They'll never get it unless they call the kettle, cattle.

JOB (definition)

You will soon find out that there are some areas of work and responsibility that, though not written down, are clearly defined. To illustrate this, a pantomime was being mounted at the London Palladium and a horse was brought on stage and promptly let loose. The Producer, Emile Littler, shouted out for the Property Master, Ronnie Harris, who popped his head from round a flat.

"Ronnie," said Mr Littler, "That horse has crapped on stage. Clear it up will you."

"Can I ask you a question Mr Littler?" enquired Ronnie. "How fresh is it?"

Mr Littler looked puzzled, "What's that got to do with anything?"

"Well," came the wise reply, "if it's warm it's Electrics, if it's cold it's Props."

JOE'S

Is the familiar diminutive for Joe Allen's, a restaurant and bar situated in the bowels of Exeter Street, off the Strand, popular with turns and those that like to stare at them.

Theatre folk are always adventuresome and willing to try anywhere new for a meal if the bill's split or someone else is paying.

So not only nightly do they throng into Joe's, but they descend on a host of others too. You'll catch them in The Ivy, Sheekey's, P.J.'s Grill, The Delaunay and... er, that's about it.

JOEY (1)

Is the nickname for a clown honouring the memory of the one and only Joe Grimaldi, The King of Clowns, who ruled at Drury Lane and Sadler's Wells at the start of the 19th century.

JOEY (2)

Is also the nickname for a young Australian kangaroo, which in turn, is also the nickname used by some for those Australian actors who can't make their minds up and keep hopping back and forth between Sydney and Adelaide.

JOSEPH

A very popular family musical which is always on somewhere. Note that its full correct title is *Joseph and the Amazing Technicolor Dreamcoat*. Such attention to detail is important for it makes a show slightly longer.

JUGS

Are nowadays wot appear on page three of the *Sun*. A Toby Jug is not in any way connected to over-developed male chests but is a decorative beer mug named after Sir Toby Belch and shaped in the likeness of famous past celebrities of fact and fiction including the occasional actor.

JUGULAR

My advice is to go for the jugular when dealing with theatre mice.

JUMPERS

Will sometimes be found on cold jugs besides being the title of a very witty play by Tom Stoppard.

Jumpers are seldom worn on stage these days. Though, if loosely knitted, they can be used for chain mail in tight-budgeted Shackspeerean productions.

JURY

After your play's first-night reviews, should you be told that the jury's out on this one, you can bet they won't return.

JUSTICE

You won't find it around much these days so best not bring it up in conversation.

Plays by Galsworthy are so dating.

JUVE

Juve is an abbreviation of Juvenile, not an expression relating to everyone's behaviour in this business but to describe a part played by a younger member of a company. If 'Juve' is followed by the word 'Lead' then you're talking Bobby or Polly in *The Boy Friend*, Exclude lead and you're talking Maisie, until she trips Polly up and takes over.

KABARET

K IS FOR:

KABARET (a)

If you're offered some one-nighters (see *One Nighters*) of a show with this title, the hard K is the giveaway that the entertainment's back to Berlin with lashings of Sin, but is NOT the Kander and Ebb classic. The other giveaway is that the first gig's the Olde Biscuit Factory, Barking. One to avoid.

KABUKI DROP (a)

Originated in the Orient but you won't have to play Tokyo to experience or practise it.

It's a double-release effect that allows a cloth, previously flown, to drop spectacularly in a second to the deck either to reveal, or if bagged up, to hide, a turn or scene.

KABUL

Another exotic venue, slightly nearer to these shores but definitely one to miss for the foreseeable future, even if your touring stage version of *Carry On Up The Khyber* went down a storm in East Anglia.

KAFTANS

So, as you can't get one from there, and you're really into retro, you'll have to find one in a charity shop.

KEY (the)

Another much-used directorial word, as in "the Key to this scene...", meaning that you've all missed the point and lost the plot.

Another key is the Key to the Grid, but between you and me, it's my firm belief that grids are never really so secured. In decades of hard searching I've yet to find one bloody key that fits or, for that matter, even a lock.

KEYBOARD (a)

There are three types of keyboards in theatre.

There's the one you'll see at the Stage Door groaning under the weight of all the mislabelled dressing-room keys.

The other two are the ones you'll trip over at some point in your career for they are the keyboards as used for rehearsals or in the pit. The first type are broken and the second semi-broken. Both categories are heavy, so, to avoid a hernia, get assistance before moving them.

KIDNAPPED BY ALIENS

Is, I consider, the best ever excuse for a non-appearance. The trouble is, spookily, that I have never heard it used. Could it be that they are here, on stage, and with us?

KILL

During a fit up, should you be in a darkened auditorium and overhear a brisk command to "kill it", nine times out of ten the lighting designer is not referring to the theatre cat but to a light. Nine times out of ten.

KILL A LAUGH (to)

Means that moment on stage when one actor destroys an audience's laughter at another actor's lines or actions by cutting in with either of his own. There are two ways of looking at this action: It's either an unforgivable malpractice or about time.

KIRBY'S FLYING BALLET

Praise be where praise is due. Actors may have been flown and lowered jerkily into productions for centuries but today's development of the art of 'invisible' flying is due to one man.

Without Joseph Kirby's inventions, Cirque du Soleil and all the others could still be horizontally stranded in their sawdust rings.

Mr Kirby was a West End Master Carpenter who in 1898 filed a patent for a drum-and-shaft-based machine that could lift actors into mid-air as if by magic.

He sprung to immediate international fame in 1904 when he was engaged to fly the first Peter Pan. It was an enormous critical and popular success despite Anthony Hope's gritty comment, "Oh, for an hour of Herod."

The flying was so realistic to the Edwardian audiences that J.M. Barrie had to alter his script to prevent children running home and setting sail from the nearest window. Since then Kirby's invention has continued to delight young audiences around the world.

It's also delighted those casts and crews who have wearied of an obnoxious Peter Pan.

Nothing's quite as satisfactory as leaving an actor dangling in mid-air with no more script to squeak.

KISMET

If you're stiff-upper-lipped you will know of course that 'Kismet' is what the dying Nelson really said to Hardy. It is a Turkish word meaning Destiny or Fate and so a most appropriate word for your new career, where, of course, success lies entirely in the lap of the Gods.

It is also the title of a musical set in Old Baghdad by Wright and Forrest. Recently revived at the Coliseum in 2007, it was described by its lead Michael Ball in an interview as "shockingly, gloriously awful... like being in a cross between *Springtime for Hitler* and *Carry On Camel.*"

Kismet has worked, though, for this singular star. He won an Olivier for *Hairspray* in 2008.

KISSING

You must learn to recite from memory the Rules of Theatrical Kissing:

1. The Producer kisses the Leading Players.
2. The Leading Players kiss each other.
3. The other players kiss themselves and sometimes kiss a Leading Player.

Once these rules are remembered, the next thing is to memorise this little ditty:

A wise old ham once declaimed, "Follow my simple tip. He who avoids a kiss from everyone, avoids the herpal lip."

KLEPTOMANIA

It is not only the world of retail that is plagued by kleptomania.

This compulsive mental disorder is rampant throughout society and the results are frankly appalling. Undertakers report stolen coffins, golf players their balls and, in our profession, actors are continually losing laughs. If they were only to look upstage they would no doubt identify the thief. Discovery sometimes leads to imitation but this should be discouraged for, if nothing else, it stretches a show's playing time.

KNAP (take the)

A variety term used when one half of an act would slap their hands together as the other half would pretend to hit them.

KNAPSTICK (a)

Is the equivalent of a slapstick, apart from the spelling.

KNIGHTS

There have been Theatrical Knights in this business since Henry Irving was so honoured in 1895. They are mostly knighted 'for services to the theatre' which should not be confused with 'servicing the theatre' which happens, of course, on a daily basis though, indeed, more often nightly.

KNOBS

On and offstage are in constant demand. Big, average or small, people are always grabbing them but if they try to grab yours, tell them loudly and clearly to 'knob off'.

At this moment the ball's firmly in your court. You can deny their entrance, make your exit, or go for broke and milk the moment for as long as you like. You're the actor whose hand's on the knob now, and it's your door turn, not theirs.

KNOCKS (Three)

Of a cane on the stage of an 18th-century French theatre were the traditional form of announcement that the show was about to begin and, to help sightlines, could the messieurs kindly remove their *chapeaux*?

KNOTS

Many knots are used backstage to secure scenery and cast when not in use.

They are tied very intricately and with great care and precision, so should you be called upon to release one suddenly, a Stanley knife is invaluable.

KRAPP

A fitting last entry to exit from the letter **K**, for it is a word you can fling into any conversation while denying it has any reference to the subject or matter under discussion.

Once seen, Samuel Beckett's character preys continually on all our subconscious minds.

LANTERN

L IS FOR:

LANTERN (the)

This is not only what the Porter in the 'Unmentionable' swings around, endangering all and sundry, but also the technical term for an aperture above the grid that can be opened or closed. The original intention was that when it was opened, all that hot air that builds up during a performance from both lights and cast could be expelled and comfort restored.

The fact that it also acted as a natural chimney if left open, let in buckets of rainwater and bloody Mary Poppins only slowly dawned; nowadays most lanterns are kept firmly locked shut and are opened solely at the discretion of the Master Carpenter. Perhaps a revival of *St Joan* will reverse the trend.

LASER

A type of acronym you'll keep well clear of now you know it stands for Light Amplification by the Stimulated Emission of Radiation.

LAWYERS

The Law and the Theatre are closely linked. Both are dependent on the written word and both use performers to express and interpret these words either in court or on stage.

If that all sounds a bit dull to you, I will only add that I have nothing more to say about theatrical lawyers as I myself cannot afford to be sued and if you put that down to excessive caution may I quote Charles Dickens: "The one great principle of the English law is, to make business for itself."

LEAD (the)

Has nothing to do with what's inside your bag when you're stopped and searched. It refers to the star of your production and should be pronounced as in Leeds without the letter S. However, this does not prevent many a Lead giving a leaden performance.

LEGITIMATE

An old-fashioned expression to differentiate serious, professional drama from the frivolity of Musicals and Variety. It is seldom used nowadays. Theatre has become pretty egalitarian in that there's really not much difference these days in the artistic and production comparison of *Lily Lays Liverpool* versus *Edna Eats Everton*, even if one does have the advantage of an Arts Council grant.

LES DAWSON

A fondly remembered, if now sadly dead, overweight, lugubrious comedian. Not to be confused with *Les Misérables*, the West End's longest running Musical.

LEVITATION

The early saints may have succeeded in this paranormal feat, but actors and technical staff only appear to float after too long a break between shows on a matinee day. If you are really keen on attempting the improbable, do so in the confines of your dressing-room. That way, should you possibly succeed, you won't sail up to the grid to coarse cries of "Rise Above it, Wendy".

LIBIDO

When you are asked to take part in a game of Libido, remember they'll know you haven't a Cluedo if you ask if it's something like Ludo. Stick to Poker.

LIES

Lies are more than common in this business but the best are always told by those who "lie through their ill-fitting teeth".

LINE (a)

Has a professional meaning as well as a social one.

Lines in our business are either (a) whole sentences that actors somehow manage to remember and recite to each other onstage (see *Stagecraft*) or (b) ropes or chords that are used to hold sets in place and to fly scenery with.

LIQUID PARAFFIN

Is the only make-up remover that can double as a laxative. Handy for both tight-budgeted actors and constipated dressers, though as the former often mark the bottles the latter will need to top them up.

LISTERINE

Even if you have taken my advice and left your halitosis at home, this doesn't mean that others will be so obliging. Bad breath is among the front-runners of the many hazards encountered in this crowded business and the only two instant remedies are chronic upstaging and Listerine. The first option will last only as long as the breadth of the set is, so it's best to concentrate on the second.

This splendid product, first formulated in 1879 by Dr Joseph Lawrence and Jordan Wheat Lambert, was originally a surgical antiseptic named after Dr Joseph Lister, who first pioneered the use of disinfectants in surgery in his operating theatre in 1865. It's been a mouthwash since 1914 and since then has been used by tens of thousands of thespians. And if that doesn't take your breath away, nothing will.

LIPSTICK

Has been worn for centuries on stage, though touched up, of course, from time to time. It first adorned the lips of male actors during the reign of Elizabeth I and had transferred to the female *labiae* shortly before Mrs Bracegirdle's retirement. It is widely used by both sexes today and is easily obtainable, unlike the product available in more ancient times. An actor wishing to bring a flush of authenticity to Cleopatra's mouth should be warned that her lippy ingredients consisted of crushed carmine beetles mixed with ants. It might be kinder to the insect world to stick to Clinique.

LOAD INS

Are American Get Ins.

LOANS

Always quote what Shackspear said when asked for one, i.e. "Neither a borrower nor a lender be."

You'll probably be called a tight-arsed git but you can reply that the quote is not from *Corialanus* and that you're in need of the loan yourself.

LONG RUNS

It has to be said Long Runs are really important, in fact vital, for the survival of the West End as we know it.

You may think that that may sound a bit dramatic, but without Long Runs, I have to warn you that we really all would be in a pretty bad place.

Just think of the consequences; a complete way of life would end. An avalanche of CCJs, child maintenance orders, credit cancellations and mortgage repossessions would bring theatre as we know it to an utter standstill if we didn't have long runs.

So the only sensible attitude is: Long May They.

LOVE

A good word to use when you can't remember someone's name. "Hello, Love" is optimistic and friendly and not too familiar unless you're talking to your Producer.

LUVVIES
(see *Actors*)

LX

This stands for Electrics. All theatres are run on electricity these days, for the use of gas has gone by way of gaiters. The advantage is that fewer theatres blow up.

Each theatre has an LX Department consisting of at least one employee, which in that case makes it hard to get your lightbulbs changed. The Department man the Lighting Board and are responsible for all the theatre's plumbing amongst many other things.

It would be correct to assume that electricity and water don't mix too well so a prudent old pro seldom turns the light on in the toilet (see *Torch*).

LYCRA

'Fat girls in lycra', say some unkind people, epitomises the strange, steamy world of sticky stage-school Sunday concerts.

The audiences are the fat girls' parents and the fat girls are the performers. This ensures that every number is a showstopper, especially when a fat girl falls into the pit.

Lycra is *de rigeur*, though please note that riggers don't wear lycra in public.

MAGIC

M is for:

MAGIC

A much-used theatrical word which some may say is overused, abused and discredited.

But though you may not trust the truth of titles of such shows as, say, the *Magic of the Music*, box-office returns usually prove that there are still enough true believers out there.

MAGICIAN

Nearly everybody who works in the theatre has the ability to be a magician. One minute they're absolutely visible on stage, and the next, when there's something heavy to lift or someone heavier to placate, they've completely gone and vanished. Just like that.

MAKE-UP

Is terribly important. Here you are in a business where so much importance is placed on personal appearances. So never be tempted yourself to apply any old blush or mascara. Make sure you book a stylist for your Top Turn.

MARIE CELESTE

Impecunious producers still dream about rediscovering this legendary missing play by the reclusive Josephine Miles. They can't resist the wonderful idea of having a cast that won't cost anything. If you point out that there's still a set to pay for they'll sulk and then cheer up, because "in my version, Darling, it's sunk". It's when you point out that their audience is just as likely to vanish that they'll order a large one and, before paying, disappear for ever into that dark night.

MARK UP/OUT

This always sorts out (if you'll excuse me, ladies) the men from the boys, for it's the first real test for all those who profess to be stage managers.

The first mark up/out in any production takes place on the splintered floor of a dirty, draughty, ill-lit hovel (see *Rehearsal Rooms*) and the ritual involved is as follows: The ground plan (see *Ground Plan)* is laid open on the floor and all present lie beside it. The DSM produces a pencil (broken) and a ruler. The ASM offers a pencil sharpener (dull) which is brushed aside by the DSM who has now found a felt-tip pen (thick).

The DSM now gets to his or her knees and, holding the ruler in both hands, glides it around the plan muttering dark calculations that are written down by the ASM over, on, or by the sides of the measured lines. This ceremony can take any amount of time, minutes or hours, though invariably the DSM's knees will suddenly collapse. This collapse causes the DSM to topple over onto the ASM with the inevitable result that the felt-tip pen tears a great big gash in the plan.

It is at this point that the DSM declares emphatically that it is time to "Mark out".

Both stand and search their bags. Several rolls of coloured tape appear, together with a crumbling piece of chalk. It is now that the DSM must make a crucial decision.

He or she will sniff the air, and glare gimlet-eyed around.

Those not visually impaired (approximately 37 percent) will be able to see if there is a window and, if there is one, which points of the compass it faces.

This is a crucial moment for the forthcoming rehearsals. Depending on which way the set is marked out, the DSM has the blatant power to leave the actors groping in the dark, or, to let the sunlight blind them at certain critical hours of the day. It's not a hard choice if you've experienced the former but I have witnessed less experienced DSMs sporting sunglasses at noon.

And now the die is cast and a long tape measure is unrolled. As the DSM chants out the list of measurements the ASMs scurry around the room placing chalk marks at salient points and, where necessary, joining said points together with their coloured tape.

Two factual points: 1) There is never enough tape; 2) The measurements never add up, let alone join up.

As the exhausted, sweat-stained team argue bitterly whether the plan is in inches or centimetres, you may well ask what is the CSM's part in all of this?

None at all if they've any sense. At least not until the dust has settled. Then they really make themselves indispensable by buying everyone a large drink (see *White Envelope*).

MARIE TEMPEST (a)

Dames of the British Theatre never like being upstaged by inadequate objects and in this case I don't mean their leading men.

Dame Marie Tempest was a 'difficult' actress, but hot box office for the first three decades of the 20th century. Her forte, in the latter part of her career, was in Drawing Room comedies and she was the original Judith Bliss in Noël Coward's *Hay Fever*.

Drawing Room comedies are curiously enough mostly set in living rooms or dining rooms and this usually entails a box set with doors to match.

A star entrance was then traditionally upstage centre, but the door on one particular box set had problems staying closed because of the rake. It would swing open prematurely before her entrance, allowing all to view her while she was adjusting her corsage, and then mischievously do the same throughout all her best dramatic moments.

At the end of yet another door-starring performance the Master Carpenter was summoned from the pub. To avoid any more tantrums and to get back to his pint he solved the problem in one: he reinforced the door hinges with screw levers and this device was named after the Dame.

They are still used to this day when all else fails, but please advise any of your actors of the slack wrist variety to butch up for once and give a good push on their entrance.

MASQUE (a)

Is not a misspelling and so is not something the Phantom wears or one of those places where you lose your shoes and bow to Mecca.

Masques were 17th-century extravaganzas. They used story lines pinched from mythology, and combined music, singing, dancing and acting. "All round entertainment" you might say, and "Can we grab one next Saturday?" but the answer these days is sadly "No dear, the Civil War finished them all off."

MASSAGE (a)

Is becoming increasingly popular amongst performers. However, it should never be encouraged during a performance despite the saying about idle hands being the Devil's work.

MASTER CARPENTER (a)

Is the head of a theatre's Stage Department. Master Carpenters have their own tools and are not afraid to use them ferociously on wayward sets.

MATELOT (bonjour)

If someone says that to you, be aware that you are west of Brest or have entered a twilight zone. French sailors haven't been seen on the legitimate West End stage since the middle of the last century.

MATTRESS

Not to be confused with Mistress (see *Wardrobe*).

Mattresses will come in useful if you are doing such plays as *Les Liasons Dangereuses* even if they are a bit grubby by the end of the run. They are also very good for breaking people's falls after a dramatic onstage exit.

If the Soprano's really pissing you off you can soften Tosca's fall from the heights of Castel Sant'Angelo by substituting a trampoline for a mattress, but make sure it's the final performance.

MD

These initials stand for Musical Director.

Musical Directors come generally in two types of tempo: quietly flamboyant or flamboyantly quiet. What they all share, you'll be glad to know, is a sense of humour even if it is just plain sadistic.

MEAL BREAKS

Everyone's entitled to meal breaks but it does not mean you have to eat with everyone or they, for that matter, with you.

MEETING (in a)

A universal euphemism for not wanting to talk to somebody.

MEMORIAL SERVICES

Are an everyday occurrence in our busy lifestyle.

They usually and thoughtfully never take place on a matinee day, so if you want to avoid one you'll have to come up with a better excuse. If, on the other hand you are up for it the rules are: Always wear a tie, never sing too loud and turn up at the right time, place and day.

MERKIN (a)

Is a pubic wig, these days no longer dimly seen on stage.

High ticket prices demand equivalent production values and modern audiences are entitled to view the real thing.

MIC (a)

Not a short, abbreviated Irishman but the single-syllable term used in theatre for the full, and, in my opinion, rather resonant word 'microphone'.

This is the age of dropped vowels and consonants, so much so that much of public speaking is oft reduced to pubic. To counter this pernicious trend and the added inability of some actors to project further than they can spit, the Sound Department was invented. Armed with the latest German hardware these audio warriors swarm about Theatreland pinning mics onto anybody who opens their mouth in a musical.

This, in theory, dramatically increases the audience's appreciation of a production, but from my experience can only be guaranteed to enhance the experience if the sound operator forgets to fade the appropriate channel after the actor has exited and decides to be grossly inappropriate.

MIRROR CURTAIN

Not for ageing chorines to admire their merkins but a unique front curtain constructed in 1822 for the Royal Coburg Theatre, or, as it is known now, the Old Vic.

The Royal Coburg had been built in the belief that it would attract a genteel audience from north of the river, but the area around Waterloo was, if you can believe this, even rougher then than it is today. The curtain was constructed of sixty-six pieces of glass. It was meant to be an irresistible novelty but it only succeeded in scaring the rowdy crowd out of their wits by giving them for once a candid view of themselves.

All efforts to lift it then failed, and the show was cancelled until it had been dismantled. Safe from further self-discovery, the mob returned to earn the theatre the reputation of a blood bucket.

Even Edmund Kean, no prude himself – his contractual requirements specified two bottles of brandy and three whores per interval – found them rough going.

At the end of a hard week in 1831 he told his last audience that, "In my life I have never acted to such a set of ignorant, unmitigated brutes as I have before me."

His successors today have unknowingly never had it so good.

MISCUE

Miscues never happen on your own shows. The culprit is 'Equipment Malfunction' which is of epidemic proportions these days as more and more equipment is added to your workload. So blame your hearing aid and the sound department for giving you the wrong batteries.

MISTER JET

When someone in the know sidles up to you in the wing and whispers hoarsely in your ear that Mr Jet's in the building, they are not suggesting that you phone the *Sun* hotline and rush around to the box office to find what seat he's in. They're telling you the code words that mean there's a fire and, however small it may be, that's serious, very, very serious.

Fire is rightly considered the theatre's Enemy No.1 by local authority officials, for they, unlike producers, have no trivial reason to fear the critics or the attractions of rival forms of artistic entertainment such as *Strictly Come Dancing* or Tate Modern.

Fire is an ancient enemy that has consumed theatres for centuries. Famous London victims of its savagery include Shakespeare's Globe in 1613 and the Theatre Royal Drury Lane, twice torched in 1672 and 1809.

The second conflagration may have destroyed the whole building despite its iron curtain, but, in compensation, it afforded its owner Richard Brinsley Sheridan the perfect riposte. Asked why he was sitting so calmly across the street in the Piazza Coffee House watching the inferno rage he replied, "May not a man be allowed to drink a glass of wine by his own fireside?"

Public safety is a paramount concern, for fire not only destroys buildings. Sadly, on 5 September 1887, one hundred and eighty-six people alone were killed in the Theatre Royal, Exeter, fire and, by an uncanny coincidence on that same day, seventy-five people were killed when the Exeter Theatre in New York burnt down.

The last theatre to be badly damaged by fire in London was the Savoy in 1990 though the Iron worked its purpose for, being in, only the auditorium was completely gutted.

So, please remember Mr Jet, and should you hear the name, take heed and action.

MODEL BOX

There's nothing saucy about a model box.

It's usually just a black cardboard scale model of a specific theatre's proscenium opening, stage area and back wall into which a set designer can place his set model to show to all interested parties. It only get's remotely saucy if he is asked to put *Snow White and the Seven Dwarfs* into an Anne Summers setting.

MONITOR

If you are told that a situation is being monitored you can be sure that no one has an earthly clue as to how to deal with it.

MOTIVATION

While the wise Michael Simkins summed it up for the actors in his indispensable book *What's My Motivation?*, other people work in other departments of theatre because they are (a) socially motivated or (b) because they are motivated socially.

For most of us employed backstage the choice, whatever your conscience or political views, is generally (a).

The second option doesn't really have a commercial look in, for you must remember that this business is one of the more successful bastions of pure dictatorship, be it in the form of a lone producer or the Arts Council's funding committee.

MOVES (1)

Are what actors do to keep the audience and themselves awake. They may have no resemblance to the blocking at all, and will afterwards be termed 'disgraceful' by other members of the cast, or 'inspirational' by the resident director who may just have happened to pop in out front to refresh his or her memory after a three-month unavoidable absence.

MOVES (2)

When a show moves it is either on tour, going from one town to another, or, if it is in the West End, transferring from one theatre to a smaller one, usually for reasons of budget.

MULTIPLE PLUGS

Are strictly banned anywhere backstage. You should confiscate them periodically from dressing rooms in order to have all sorts of devices humming away in your office at the same time.

MUSICALS

It's a popular misconception to believe that Musicals are a 20th-century addition to the theatrical canon.

The first English musical, as we think of the form today, was *The Beggar's Opera* written by John Gay, which was put on at Lincoln's Inn

Fields in 1728 by John Rich. It was an instant success and, as they said at the time, "made Gay rich and Rich gay".

Musicals generally place great reliance on music and lyrics though there are those that buck the trend and opt for sets and costumes.

If you are going to specialise in this form of entertainment it is essential to take Musical Theatre very seriously for it is a very serious business.

Musicals nowadays are terribly important to the economy of the country and the well-being of our citizens. Millions have been uplifted, inspired, some even cured by tunes that have entered every second household's collective consciousness.

And every first household? It's either an empty second home or the inhabitants are out at a Care in the Community Centre.

MUSICIANS

Every Musical has to have them, unless the show's from any other EU country bar the UK.

MYOPIA

If someone tells you that their excuse for the day is because they are shortsighted, scare them by telling them that it can lead to Myopia.

If they look blank and ask where that is, tell them you flew.

MYSTERIES (The)

Or Mystery Plays were medieval religious performances based on episodes of the Bible. They were open-air, large-scale productions of a size and time scale that would have satisfied Cecil B. de Mille. The York, Wakefield and Coventry cycles were revived in the last century but these productions do take considerable time to mount so while you are waiting for the next one you may have to guess the ending of *The Mystery of Edwin Drood*, or just tickle yourself with the Misteries, the complete if abridged Mr Men collection, coming to a playhouse near you.

NAFF

N IS FOR:

NAFF

Is a term used for other people's appalling taste; never your own appalling taste in other people.

NAME DROPPING

You're going to meet all sorts of famous people in this game; however, everybody outside the game only wants to know you to know who you've worked with, so remember there are two golden rules: Most famous people these days are only famous for all of two days so don't hoard them and thus avoid those blank looks and yawns; If you're going to drop a name get it right – or as Victor Spaghetti once told me, make it flounce.

NAMES

Following on, it must be explained that there are two types of names.

The capital-lettered Names whom producers and press agents insist on inviting to First Nights under the time-honoured belief that their photographs in the next day's free newspapers may boost ticket sales. Then there are the names of your co-workers. A very good tip is to remember them, that is if you still retain that facility. It is all very hard work. There are thousands of names and hundreds of them go in and out of fashion every decade even if all are initially chosen with love and care. A popular name at the moment, for example (for young male ASMs), is 'Jason'.

This name is not only a reference to that classical Hero and his Golden Fleece, but indeed has strong modern links to sheep-shagging, unproven of course, unless said ASM's parents own up and admit to their adolescent addiction to *Neighbours*.

Young female ASMs are mostly spared the name 'Kylie' because that's such a gay thing.

NEMESIS

Never forget that Greek Goddess hovers over all who work in the theatre.

NEMO

Is the name of Jules Verne's submarine captain and comes from the Latin word meaning, of course, 'Nobody'. Useful when signing petitions.

NEPOTISM

Or "Keep it in the Family" is a fine old theatrical tradition that thrives to this day and is neither medically nor morally frowned upon.

NERO

A much-maligned Roman Emperor who, though possibly debauched and certainly matricidal, had a soft spot for the arts and the theatre in particular.

Being a self-proclaimed god he could do the imperial lot: he sang, he danced, he acted, he played the lyre and even as he committed suicide stuck to his belief of being a good old all-round entertainer. His last recorded words were: *"Qualis artifex pereo!"* ("Dead! And so great an Artist!")

NEVER

Is not a word much heeded in our business. It's really no good wagging a stern if bitten finger and moaning to the assembled company that they should NEVER be off, late, jealous, libidinous, intemperate, et cetera. It never works.

However, it's advisable to heed the word when it prefixes the following actions.

Never whistle on stage.

Never play downstage of a goldfish.

Never sport a peacock's feather about your person.

Never wear another player's left silk sock.

Never rehearse the curtain call before the dress rehearsal.

Heed these cautions and thus avoid the fate of countless others whose careers have been blighted, cursed, even abruptly ended by their refusal to believe such ancient sayings.

And now don't say you have NEVER been forewarned...

NIGHTMARES

Nightmares are very common in this job.

They come at you without warning when you are at your most vulnerable and leave you feeling exhausted and covered in sweat.

The sad thing is that they are not confined to one department, so you can bump into them all over a theatre. The best defence is to keep moving with the excuse that you've got to talk to the next.

NOTICE (the)

Happens to all shows, past, present and future. It is when the management informs the cast in writing by means of a notice on the board that the production will close on a certain date. The minimum notice allowed is two weeks. There is no maximum. Either way it's a melancholy moment and one often greeted with heartfelt despair.

"Bloody show's closing three weeks after that job I was after." Amen.

NUDITY

If still considered a bit of an onstage rarity in commercial theatre is paradoxically commonplace backstage.

Many Musical twirlies, still environmentally unaware, do their bit to raise global warming all around them by taking off their costumes at any opportunity in a vain effort to stay cool.

Equity, of course, rightly has a full-page schedule in its Agreement concerning the regulations governing nudity and simulated sex. The rules apply, however, only to what goes on on stage. Continuous backstage nudity may be an unregulated problem for some of my readers, but I can reassure them that sex of a simulated nature, as opposed to the real thing, never happens our side of the iron.

OASIS

O IS FOR:

OASIS

When you become a CSM you should try to make your Company Office a welcoming Oasis at certain times of the day. A peaceful and serene atmosphere is most attractive to all and means that once you are sure everyone else is in there, you can slip off unnoticed and be away about your business.

OFF

The list of things that can go off in a theatre are endless, but the most common are milk left in fridges and actors. Milk, by its odour, is traceable, but an actor, once he has phoned in 'off', completely vanishes.

OFF (to be)

Is the expression used on the show report when an actor misses his entrance. They will say something else.

OFF BROADWAY

A term to describe those New York theatres and plays not regarded as mainstream commercial houses or ventures.

Many Off Broadway productions have transferred to great universal success so if you want to be more sure of having a unique theatre experience (you and twenty other empty seats) you may have to venture further afield to an Off Off Broadway show.

OFFS

Is an alternative list to the 'Ons'. In Musicals, it is usually longer than the 'Ons' and grows even longer as shows mellow, age and reach Saturday night.

OFFSTAGE

Means all the areas next to the stage but invisible to the audience. They are often quite dark but it is advisable not to shine your torch around, as its beam can be distracting for those both on stage and off and can put them off their stroke.

OLD PRO (he's an)

A compliment bestowed on an actor who, regardless of age or experience, keeps his nerve while all the rest of the cast and set of *Dry Rot* collapse, and by sheer instant professionalism and the ability to play all parts plus the scenery, saves the show.

OLIVIERS (the)

Are a star-studded award ceremony where statuettes of Larry are handed over by the Great and Good and received with the utmost sincerity and humility by the Great and Good.

This event is closely watched by the Great and Good and of course, those theatrically bent.

ON SALES

Are tickets purchased by punters who then find that due to a dire emergency, the World Cup for example, they are unable to attend even a half turn of *A Voyage Around My Father*.

The tickets are then optimistically taken back to the Box Office where they are put on sale on a 'cash only' offer; strictly after all other seats have gone. For most shows, the chances of them being sold are as good as England winning.

ON STAGE

Means exactly that, be whatever's on stage: animal, vegetable or mineral.

ON THE ROAD

Is another term for being on tour. Tours, like roads, can be major or minor, ranging from large Musicals that can lumber for years around the country to nimble one-night stands with Darcey Bussell.

ON THE STICK

Has nothing to do with a French loaf unless a very short-sighted conductor is waving one in lieu of his usual baton.

ONE NIGHT STAND

Is in stage language not only what ordinary folk try to get up to on a Friday night. One Night Stands in our business also mean getting into a different venue on every night of the week, giving a performance and then moving on to the next, in other words, the Theatre of Exhaustion.

ONS

Refers to the Ons List, which means a nightly list of who's playing a cover role, but not with whom.

OP

Stands for Opposite Prompt (see *PS*).

OPENING COLD

It used to be that a producer of a new play destined for the West End would often send it out on a short tour so that any problems with script or cast could be ironed out before the Press Night in London. If they didn't, this was known as 'opening cold' as opposed to being gently warmed up in Brighton, Billingham or Bath.

Nowadays the sheer cost of production means that many shows open frigid.

OPENING NIGHT

Is also known as Press Night. Not because the auditorium and bars are uncomfortably full, but because the press and the critics are in attendance. Both the press and the critics write about the evening but the odds are that the press will be kinder.

OPERA

Operas are generally longer running than other forms of theatre but that's because they're mostly very old and have lengthy intervals.

OPERA BOUFFE

A lighter form of opera, started by the composer Hervé, whose real name was Florimond Ronger and who began his musical career as an organist in a lunatic asylum.

OPERETTA

The lightest of the trio, epitomised by Offenbach's *La Belle Hélène* and Franz Lehar's *The Merry Widow*, though both parts are sometimes sung by heavyweight sopranos.

OPPOSITION

When somebody senior to you with whom you're working asks you how the opposition's doing, they're referring not to the Labour Party, but to the rest of the West End's business.
    Always give a vague but pessimistic reply. It always cheers them up.

ORCHESTRA

A posh band.

ORPHAN

Theatrical 'orphans' appear in such shows as *Oliver!* and *Annie* and are always good for business. The more you cram on stage, the more tickets their families buy.

OSCAR (an)

Not to be confused with an Olivier, this is the Hollywood Film Award.

OSTEOPATHS

Can hurt. If you really think you have to use one, send someone else first to check them out.

OUT FRONT

When a CSM says they are going 'Out Front' it means that they are going into those areas beyond the pass door where, strictly speaking during a performance, no one else from backstage is allowed to venture.

It could be anywhere from the betting shop to the knocking shop but that's entirely up to choice.

PACK

P IS FOR:

P45s

Are issued by the accountants to employees who leave a show or when the show comes to an end. As they are official and cannot be reproduced don't use them as beer mats.

P60s

Are again issued by the accountants at the end of each tax year to show the Inland Revenue what everyone's managed to earn. They are also rather difficult to replace so make sure that your own at least is safe and dry.

PACK (of flats)

If you are working on a play with more than one set you may occasionally come across a pack in the Scene Dock or offstage. The flats are stacked together vertically and in an order that will make it easy for them to be braced and cleated together when they are brought on stage for the scene or interval change. That's the theory but, like an opened deck of cards, you may find they've been shuffled.

PANTOMIME

You must have seen one of these, haven't you? Oh yes you have!

There are roughly 200 pantos produced each year so your chances of employment are high, but always take the front end of the horse.

Yes, ASMs may well have to put in an appearance but that's all part of the fun isn't it? Oh No...? Oh yes it is!

Remember, though, even if you don't have time to have loads of fun, chances are you'll have loads of funny stories.

PAPARAZZI

Are the scum of the earth, but remember if they can chase after Lady Gaga, Lily Allen et al. they can also chase after you.

So, if you're short of gelt and really up for a taxi snog with your Top Turn, be sure they know first (the paparazzi), but always ask for cash.

PAPER THE HOUSE (to)

Is not a panto phrase but one which means that when full-looking houses are demanded, comps are duly distributed.

PART (a)

An actor's part is strictly personal to himself and only the actor should play it.

PASSAREL (a)

Is a walkway in front of the orchestra pit. This is not a permanent feature of an auditorium but is part of the scenic design of a show. It has a double usage: casts can run, dance and crawl around it and audiences can rest their feet, offspring and handbags on it.

PASS DOOR

Every theatre with a proscenium arch and iron has a pass door that allows direct access from the front of house to backstage and vice-versa without you ever having to brave the elements. This is the door through which a CSM flits between crisis and chaos.

PAUSE (to)

Is, of course, a natural occurrence in every walk of life and one that increases remorselessly with age. Everyday things in life, crossing the road, paying your tax, remembering your nearest and dearest's name, all require a necessary pause or two. This type of pause is, however, quite different from the theatrical variety as practised by actors. They use pauses for deliberate dramatic effect, or will claim so if prompted (see *Prompt*).

This tradition of non-delivery goes back into the mists of theatrical memory. In the 18th century one of the greatest champions of the pause was Charles Macklin. He had perfected the art of three different pauses, "the moderate, the long and the grand". Such was his dedication to the ability of "keeping your audience guessing", that when a prompter had the temerity to interrupt a "grand" pause, Macklin strode to the wing and, to wild applause, knocked the culprit to the ground.

The pause has never gone out of fashion and can be viewed these days wherever a Pinter (see *Harold*) play is being presented.

PENCIL

You should always use a pencil when writing important notes.

That way, should any spillage occur, the message will remain clear and legible. However, pencils should not be used on cheques, unless you are lending one of your own to someone else to write you one.

PEPPER'S GHOST

Has nothing to do with the Beatles but is an illusion using plate glass and lighting. Originally invented in 1862 by Henry Dircks and adapted for the stage by 'Professor' Pepper, it was first shown in 1862 at the Royal Polytechnic as the 'Ghost Illusion'. It was a huge success for many years and can still be seen today at several of the Disney resorts.

PERFORMANCE SUPPORT STAFF

If you see this crisp new sign on a dressing-room door it does not mean that the room will be littered with ancient actors demanding adjustment to their trusses from a single harassed nurse. In the second decade of this new century we are all categorised as being worthy of this title, each and every one of us doing our utmost to ensure that all aspects of a performance are supported. So please open the dressing-room door as slowly and carefully as possible. This will ensure that not too much injury occurs to any of the massed ranks of technicians squashed inside and will avoid you having to call out the Life Support Unit.

PERFORMERS
(see *Turns*)

PETTY CASH

Is a most serious subject and an item not to be frivolously dismissed as 'an interest free loan'. Petty, of course, derives from the French *petit* meaning small and Cash comes from the Latin *Ca...*

PHONING IN

Is what your cast do when they are going to be 'off'. Do not expect them to turn up in person to tell you, no matter how well they feel.

PHYSIOTHERAPY

Can be said to fulfil a double vital role in this business: It helps the speedy recovery of members of the cast who have suffered accidents or injuries on stage in their constant pursuit of professional perfection; and it keeps many Australians in work and off the streets.

PICK UP

Pick ups happen in theatre from the moment the curtain goes up.

That's when the actors on stage, on discovering that they almost outnumber the audience, pick up the pace.

Poignant pauses are forgotten and the action fairly zips along until the next announced or expected entrance when silence and a state of suspended animation envelop the stage.

The audience have just picked up their programmes to check if it's the interval when there comes the sound of angry chaos from the wings.

The missing actor, unable in his panic to open the set's door, takes a running jump and smashes his way in.

The stage management rush on stage and pick up firstly the stricken door and then the fallen actor (see *Priorities, Technical*).

The latter, despite mild concussion, picks up his cue and the scene springs into life. Unfortunately the follow spots are unable to pick up the actor with their lights. Not only is he singing the wrong number from the wrong show but his erratic movements are impossible to follow.

Sadly, before anyone is able to diagnose severe concussion, he falls dramatically into the pit.

The show is abandoned, and soon there is just a near-empty auditorium peopled only by a few conscientious attendants left to pick up abandoned rubbish for a fixed fee.

PINEAPPLE

There is a school of thought that believes that a pineapple is very good for the throat. If you're of that school, please remember to slice it first.

PIT (the)

Is exactly what it sounds like and if I add that it is where the musicians in a Musical lurk to play, you may understand why few, apart from them, ever venture there.

PLACES

Is the American term for Beginners. Two syllables, short and sharp to the ear, but this does not necessarily guarantee that companies the other side of the pond will be any earlier on stage.

PLAY (a)

In case you are in any doubt, a play is a show in which the spoken word is paramount. That's if you can hear it over the sound-effects and incidental music.

PLAYERS

Appear not only in plays but also in Musicals, though not at the same time, unless they are a fleet of foot and walking understudies, and department stores when they are not appearing elsewhere.

PLOT (the)

Has nothing to do with losing the plot, which, of course, we all routinely do.

The plot is the story of the play and is useful to have (but not guaranteed) before you go into rehearsals. Plays can be quite complicated and those that are thrillers have all sorts of twists and diabolically clever explanations; however, storylines in Musicals are, and should be, simple, so as to be in harmony with their audiences.

POLARI

If an actor comes up to you and says: "Varder the bona willets on that dolly palone!" you've just been addressed by that very rare specimen, a heterosexual speaker of Polari.

This pot-pourri language is a heady mix of Romany, Yiddish, Italian and English mixed up with rhyming slang and back slang. It's still used here and heard there, even if the most famous exponents were undoubtedly that fictional radio duo, Julian and Sandy, who both sadly clocked their batts years ago.

PORT

Is excellent for actors' throats. Always keep a bottle in the Company Office but may I recommend the White rather than the Tawny to avoid stains on dress shirts, nightshirts, hair shirts or any other that you, or they, may be wearing. Whatever, even if it all goes dramatically wrong, you should take comfort from that old nautical/hemp-house saying: "Any port in a storm."

PORTAL (s)

"Close the portals!" is a cry which will come familiar to you as casts decrease and costs increase.

A portal is a dark flat attached to a permanent show leg that can be slid on stage to concentrate and focus the audience's attention to the scene being played.

It is part of that whole trick that makes up a rare theatrical commodity: an economical success.

PR

Stands for Press Representative. A PR is essential if your show is going to get any free publicity and paper coverage as opposed to buying ads on television or by the page.

PRs believe quite rightly that a Top Turn's 'statement of belief in the show' on *Songs of Praise*, or their revelations in the 'How I Masticate My Food" column in *Health and Hormones Magazine*, is very important. For a CSM, of course, this can cause havoc with the rehearsal schedule. Do, however, take consolation in the knowledge that a PR will dish you all the best dirt and never bother you again after Press Night.

PRACTICALS

Are things that actually work on stage, such as a switch on a desktop light. That is, of course, if no one's stolen the lightbulb.

PREMIERE

Equates to First Night but is strictly movie-speak. If your producer uses it in conversation he may not be aware that his actors are live on a nightly basis. On the other hand he may have a point.

PRESDIGITATORS

You'll be hard pressed to see these card manipulators now in theatres. They're more likely to pop up next to your table at a restaurant and ruin a perfectly good meal by flashing a Royal Flush.

PRESET (the)

The preset happens before each show when the stage management and crew restore props, furniture and set to their starting-point, cleaning up any mess that they or the cast may have made from the show before.

PRESS CUTTINGS

Are not to be confused with pressed cuttings of the type that your dear Aunt Doris collects from hedgerows to slip into Uncle Dexter's tea in the continual hope that they'll be the death of him.

Press cuttings are vital for the self-esteem of members of this profession. Without them they become shadowy wraiths, akin to Enoch Soames.

My advice for you is to obtain and cherish every single column inch of reviews, profiles, and exposures. They will be of great, if yellowing, consolation in your twilight years.

However, I must give some words of warning. Please be cautious with their storage. I would strongly suggest that all press-cutting books be arranged vertically in low, open shelves and never consigned haphazardly and horizontally to high cupboards.

A dear friend, who had chosen the second storage option, was recently entertaining some young admirers. Wishing to impress them, he threw open the cupboard door with a grand gesture, and was crushed to death by his collection.

PREVIEWS

Are performances that take place before the First Night. They are important for actors in straight plays for it gives them the time to have a fair chance to better or even remember their lines. Musical Theatre is another matter. The general rule for Musical Previews is that the first will be cancelled or curtailed due to that old and trusted standby 'Technical Difficulties'.

There is no need for CSMs to take this personally at all. It doesn't refer to them, and if difficulties are truly technical, the efforts to overcome them add up to a nice little overtime earner.

Once technical difficulties are resolved by a fresh script or score, new actors or a replacement director, the second preview can safely get under way and all is plain sailing till, of course, the next morning when the whole process of 'reinterpretation' starts again.

PRG

Stands, of course, for persons of restricted growth, whom you may encounter in December when they are out and about and up to no good with Snow White.

PRINCE

Harry and William are not known to be consistent theatregoers but Uncle Edward is most supportive.

PRODIGAL/PRODIGIOUS

These are similar-sounding words and ones often used when talking up this business. However, you must be able to differentiate between them. By way of example, always remember the fate of the spectacular *Ben-Hur on Ice.*

It may very well have been prodigious in its size and grandeur but the producers were truly prodigal with the outstanding talent of Brent Cruise who fleetingly played the eponymous hero.

Minor cost cuts led to a major catastrophe. The ice melted, the galley sunk and Ben-Hur and his fellow slaves failed to surface at the sudden end of Act One.

The only consolation was that a hitherto limp performance by the wicked Messala (Peter Coy) was never put to the chariot test in Act Two.

PRODUCER

Most people, in or out of this business, have a very muddled and misguided conception of what a producer is, or for that matter, does.

They seem to imagine them on a typical day, in next year's Paul Smith suit, sitting in the back of Stephen Fry's taxi, shouting into a hands-free while their PA pours them their second Bloody Mary.

That's, of course, before that power breakfast at the Wolseley when their morning really takes off.

By lunchtime, they believe, the Producer will have typically negotiated the rights to *Die Hard 1 to 4 - the Musicals*, and, if that meal's in Paris, persuaded Johnny Depp to consider a short season at the Albert

Hall in a ninety-minute adaptation of *À la Recherche du Temps Perdu* – if Trevor Nunn can find time to possibly direct.

Should the Chinook be on standby they'll make the third race at Ascot by a nose and soak up whatever's on offer before their early evening's 'prowl' round the dressing rooms, box offices and bars of their current West End hits.

As soon as 'Curtain Up!' hits the Avenue, they'll be dashing off to Dino's newly opened 'Dementia' for a 'development' meeting with the architects of 'Dachshunds', their new multi-theatre complex on the Isle of Dogs. After that it's off to Boujiis and...

How wrong they bloody are!

Real producers breakfast frugally on porridge and prune juice, before endless, joyless meetings with HMRC.

Lunch is a bagel-less, sugar-free affair with their mothers, followed typically by a solid afternoon's perusal of *What's on the Curriculum for 2012?* in order for them to selflessly arrive at a sensible and caring solution to the correct choice for their next Shaykesparien venture.

The daily workouts at the gym are never publicised, nor those continual steady, charitable handouts dispensed to those in this profession who have been quite forgotten by all their other fellow workers.

Having quietly seen 'Curtain Down' it's back to the office to deal with rewarding correspondence from The Actors' Church Reunion, before tackling a few uplifting scripts, a glass of camomile tea, a traditional glance in the mirror and then, at last, a softly sighed "Goodnight Sweet Prince."

The entry for Producer has been kindly sponsored by SOLT.

PRODUCTION DESKS

In musical theatre proliferate during production periods. Though they are of a uniform design – square-cut sheets of ply, wide enough to rest over two rows of seats – they fairly jostle for position.

The first ones out in the stalls are the Production Manager's and the Lighting Designer closely followed by all the other technical departments.

But then the rest of the creative team arrive and rehearsals have been known to be abandoned until their production desks arrive to join the starting line.

Soon the stalls are completely littered with them, lined up and ready for the off, all buzzing with activity as their occupants eat, drink and check their emails from one another.

It is often very hard to find a clear pathway through the aisles and one must be particularly wary when approaching an abandoned production desk. Odds are that the occupant will be slumbering beneath it and will not appreciate being walked over even if he is the author.

Luckily these vital workstations only have a limited lifespan in the greater scheme of things, for sure enough, at some point, the show actually has to open and start earning money to pay for their hire.

PRODUCTION MANAGERS

Are the backstage jugglers of this business. They catch the budgets, big or small, that producers throw at them and keep them somehow up in the air; or at least, the majority of them do.

Those that don't, it could be said, drop their balls. Remember, it's a very hard job driving all the technical departments forward at synchronised time in the countdown to the First Night. That is why most production managers have loud voices which can be raised at times to cut clean across the endless racket of mobile phone calls, video games, pole dancing et cetera to encourage all and sundry to "Bloody get on with it."

PROFESSIONAL

This title is liberally awarded in the Theatre, for the simple reason that there are very many of us who are entitled to it.

After all, the vast majority of people working in this profession are dedicated and disciplined and fully deserving of all the diplomas and degrees they detail in their CVs.

However, another key factor determines whether or not this epithet can be bestowed: Do you get paid for what you do? If not, you're a poor bloody amateur, mate.

PROMENADE PERFORMANCE

A production of fluid dramatic movement and one that can range around an entire building with the spectators following or encountering the players. This type of theatre can be very visually exciting until cast and audience lose each other and respectively end up on the roof and in the basement.

PROMPT (a)

Is whenever whoever is on the Book has to feed an actor 'the word' when it appears that they have forgotten their line.

It is an unenviable task, for a prompt is never graciously received. The actor will invariably accuse the prompt of ruining their pause or berate them for not speaking clearly.

The best defence is that of non-commitment.

Actor: And here, I'd like to say... er... oh... ah... bugger. Prompt.
Prompt: Prompt what?
Actor: My line.
Prompt: OK (*rustle of pages*) right, what is it?
Actor: It's... mine – you idiot!
Prompt: No... (*rustle of script again*) Sorry. That's wrong.

PROMPT BOX (a)

Used to be a hole in the stage, down stage centre, hidden from the audience by an upright cowl where the prompter would stand with said script and deliver unsaid lines. Nowadays it's more likely to be an up-to-the minute ASM or understudy.

PROMPT COPY (the)

Is, of course, the proper title for the Book. It doesn't, of course, make it any more accurate.

PROMPT CORNER

This is where the DSM stands, sits or crouches depending on degrees of physical disability. There is usually a shelf handy on which can be put the Prompt Copy or something slightly more up-to-the-minute. It helps if the DSM can see the stage from the Prompt Corner, but this is never a god-given right or design fact.

Prompt Corners have historically nearly always been situated on the left side of the stage. This is because most actors traditionally suffer from poor hearing in their right ears.

If the Prompt Corner should be on Stage Right or OP, it is known as a Bastard Prompt. This, of course, is what the actors have always said when they cannot hear their prompt.

PROMPT SIDE

Or, as it is known by its initials, PS is another expression for Stage Left.

Stage Left is also, on average, the best wing to work unless you have a bastard prompt. Nearest to the dressing rooms, warmed by the soft glow of the prompt desk, furnished with prop tables and chairs it has a comforting congenial atmosphere compared to the often distant, dark and draughty Stage Right.

PROPERTY MASTER (a)

This ancient title derives from the days of David Garrick, who was the first producer to provide his cast with costumes rather than making them wear their own clothes on stage.

However, knowing full well his fellow actors, he had labels bearing the legend 'Property of the Management' sewn into each costume to prevent them ending up in hock at Ye Old Pawn Shoppe.

The role of Property Master thus came into being, but as most were unfamiliar with soap and water, the care of costumes was soon handed over to the Wardrobe Mistress. The Property Master was left to make and maintain all the other properties of the management used on stage such as croquet sticks and cannon balls, and these vital aids of the actors' trade in turn became known as props.

Sadly, the position has been taken over to a large extent by stage management and the title lives on only in Opera or in large theatre organisations such as The National.

Gone are the golden, olden days when every theatre company had one and the Property Master could make a steady living, plane in hand, turning out teak and mahogany dildos to specific order.

PROP MAKERS

When shows have got a sufficient budget a delightful person, wafting of perfume or gin, will turn up one day at your elbow. It's either the work-experience girl or the prop maker. Good Prop Makers can either source what's required or really do what their title says. If they can't, they know a man who can. The greater the challenge the more they like it, so it's always fun to put in a request for a stuffed ostrich or two the next time you're doing a Strindberg.

PROPS

Nowadays, Props are all those things that are used on stage by actors and break.

Besides breakage, the usual rule of Three Bs and an S should be applied:

On cheap productions they are begged or borrowed.
On classy shows they are bought.
On average, at the end they're stolen.

PROP TABLE (a)

Is often found in either wing. It will not collapse when you place your props on it, as it is practical as well as a prop table.

PUBS

Can be seen as an extension of theatre; for wherever there's a theatre you'll find one, two or half a dozen all vying for your public's and company's trade.

Some are particularly handy on Previews and First Nights, both for the intervals, when the crush is too great for your friends to get to the theatre bars, and before shows, so you'll know where to find any missing members of the cast, lighting designers, producer et cetera.

PUNCH (1)

No matter how provoked you are, you should never punch anybody in the theatre, be they audience or colleague.

Wait till you get them outside.

PUNCH (2)

A warming drink, wine-based, fortified with any handy spirits and found in foyer bars around the Christmas period.

PUNCH (3)

Is one of our most enduring theatrical characters, even if he is one of our shortest. His first recorded appearance in England was on 9 May 1662 when that ardent theatregoer Samuel Pepys espied him in Covent Garden. He is of Italian origins for his first incarnation was as Pulchinella in the 16th-century *Commedia dell'Arte* and ever since then he has been delighting audiences both young and old with his anarchic devilry.

PYROTECHNICS

Always help a show end with a bang. However, if you are going to use them in the 'Let's Blind the Audience' sense, it's best to employ a firm such as Pandemonium to organise them and, as the instructions on the box state, stand well back.

The other type is, of course, of the backstage variety and is usually sparked off by some sore, sour turn at the end of a run. The rule is that it will all end in tears so my advice is to open the Kleenex and the windows and listen to it all spill out from the comfort of another dressing-room.

Q IS FOR:

Q

Is one of those initials that you will see in prompt books and stands for Cue if you're into snooker or Q if you're into theatre.

Qs are numbered 1 to infinity in the order of their happening, for they denote a technical beginning, middle or end of a theatrical time, mood or place.

If it has the prefix LX it refers to a Lighting Q by which, and on the giving of the order, the lighting states on stage change, be it ever so subtle.

Again, should it have the prefix Sound, this again indicates a different sound effect from the one expected.

Finally, if you read the words 'Q Scene Change', you'll probably just have time to get on stage to do one.

QATAR

The Qatar National Theatre was originally opened in 1982 and was refurbished in 2005 to some very high levels of technology. It hosts a large number of shows throughout the year from visiting European companies and artists from the Gulf area including the Doha Players. The auditorium seats 550 plus the Emir.

QUAIL (a)

Is a small short-tailed game bird of the partridge family. Wild quail are far tastier than those bred for food. When killed, they should never be allowed to turn high before eating. Not to be confused with the actor Anthony Quayle (see *Spelling*) who too has sadly passed on.

QUARREL (a)

Is an everyday occurrence in the theatre. Usually of short duration, it should never be taken 'on stage' by any players in any production featuring, knives, swords, guns or toothpicks.

QUARTER (the)

Is another of those traditional calls inside the Half. Its full title is the Quarter of an Hour and that places it, in real time, twenty minutes before Curtain Up.

QUASIMODO

They don't make bell-ringers like this anymore, in fact they never did.

Victor Hugo created the hunchback for his epic novel *Notre Dame de Paris* in 1831, inspired possibly by a Monsieur Trajan who was one of the stonemasons working on the restoration of the cathedral. Hugo's book had a huge cast of characters and became an international success, but it was Lon Chaney and Charles Laughton who transformed *le bossu* from a secondary character into the star he is today, outshining even his adored Esmeralda. The story has been turned into opera, ballet and musicals.

Before the French Revolution of 1789, Notre Dame had twenty bells, which no doubt accounted for Quasimodo's deafness. All were melted down for cannon apart from the great 13-ton Bourdon Emmanuel, cast in 1681 and delivering a pure F sharp. Their Second Empire replacements, inferior in tone, are now in turn to be replaced and a new set hung cast to the original tubular quality. It is planned that they will toll out for the first time on Palm Sunday 2013. Quasimodo would be most pleased.

QUEEN (the)

Her Majesty only attends the theatre when she absolutely has to, unlike all the others who can't seem to ever keep away.

QUESTORS (the)

The Questors Theatre in Ealing, West London is the largest community theatre in Europe. It was founded in 1929 and thrives today with over 1500 members. Michael Green was a member from 1953 and his experiences on stage there led in 1962 to one of the funniest books on the world of amateur theatricals, *The Art of Coarse Acting*.

QUICK CHANGES

Can sometimes be the theatrical equivalent of the Charge of the Light Brigade. An actor bids a nonchalant farewell to his fellow players on stage, saunters off and then gallops towards the quick-change tent, bowling over anyone in his path. Dressers sprint to intercept him. They and the actor are soon a flailing mass of arms and legs. Shouts, cries and curses ring out, punctuated by the steady sound of Velcro being ripped and zips zipped as he is pushed and pummelled into a new costume.

The change is done in all of twenty seconds, allowing time for the dressers to climb shakily to their feet and for the actor to check himself in the mirror and discover that he's absolutely in wrong frock.

QUICK STUDY (a)

Is a term for an actor whose memory is such that he can retain not only entire words but whole scripts at a cursory glance. Authors' admiration can soon turn to loathing if it turns out that his memory, though broadly thorough, is intimately inaccurate.

QUINTESSENTIAL

This word is usually matched with PERFORMANCE, though one has to ask: If there are truly so many, why are there not more Theatrical Awards to accommodate them?

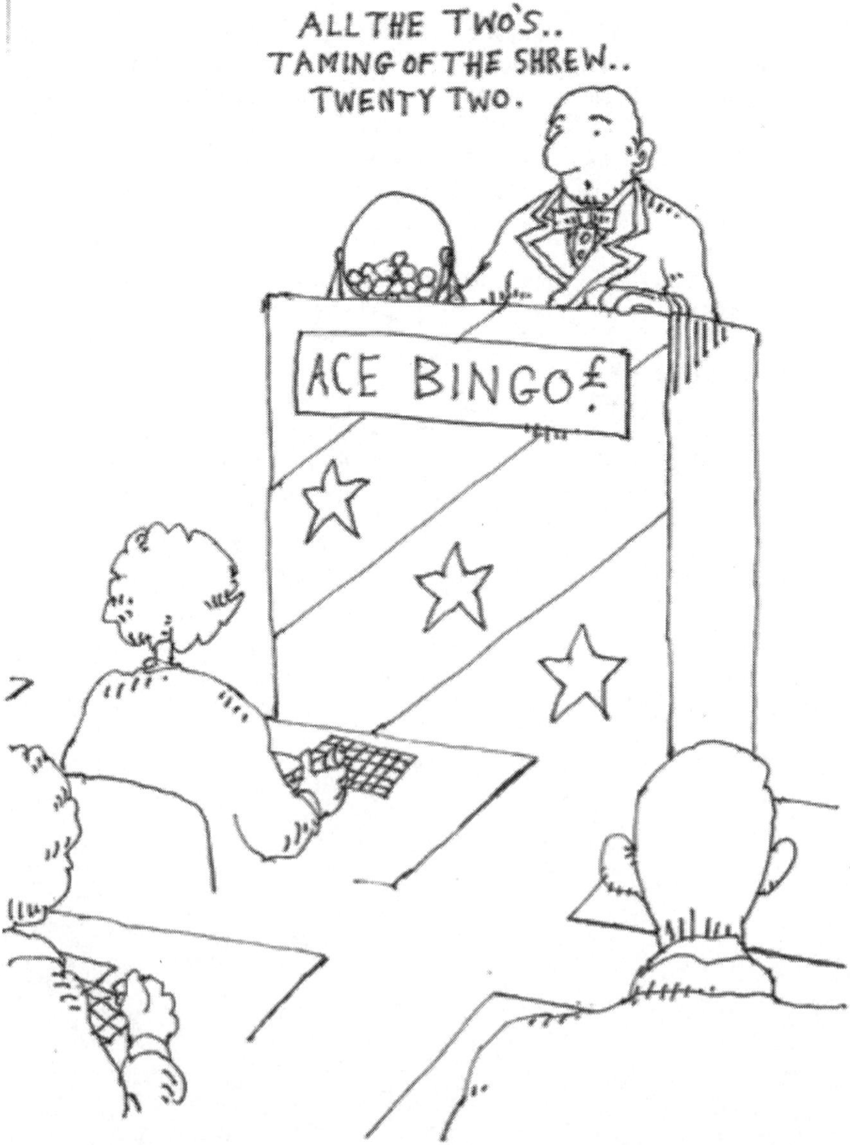

RADA

R IS FOR:

RADA (the)

Stands neither for Real Actors Do Articulate nor Rough Actors Don't Act.

The consonants and double vowel do, however, favour the former for they are the proud initials of the Royal Academy of Dramatic Art. It is, they'll have you know, the only drama school that should be prefixed with 'The', some say by royal decree.

RAG (the)

Is another name for the house curtain. Not to be confused with rug which is slang, of course, for a wig of the more obvious variety.

RAKE

Many of our older theatres have rakes. These are sloped floors, varying in the severity of the degree, stretching downwards from the back wall of the stage to the footlights.

They were originally put in to help foster the illusion of perspective but can play havoc with both scenery and ankles. To counter this, new sets incorporate level stage floors which are placed on top of the rakes. Auditoriums are also generally raked. This is to enable persons of restricted growth to have a rare, unimpeded view of life through the fourth wall.

RATS

Whatever they say, rats are getting fairly common backstage. If your cast say they've seen one and the FOH manager comes to you with his usual line of "Just mice here, dear", don't be fooled and be prepared to deal routinely and calmly with such vermin. To do so accurately, it is always useful to borrow that loaded airgun from the Company Office (see *CM Essential Equipment*).

READ THROUGH (the)

Is the sixth thing that happens on the first day of rehearsals soon after everyone's had coffee and announced, with varying degrees of confidence, who they are and what they do. After any obvious fakes have been expelled, the director asks everyone to gather round the model of the set. The designer should be on hand to explain its intricacies – that's if he hasn't severed an artery while assembling it. Finally, the cast are arranged on chairs set in a circle and then the read through of the script commences. Always stay until you are certain that the right play has been distributed and then you can slip away on an appropriate cough.

READING BETWEEN THE LINES

Any actor with an ounce of intelligence is naturally tempted to do this. However, beginners should be warned that it is an exercise fraught with danger.

As you study the text, it may become clearer as to what the symbolism of Pozzo's bald head beneath that bowler hat really represents, but it may equally mean that when blind instinct makes you suddenly pick up your weapon and rush to deal with events at hand, you are not only late for your entrance but enter not with a harpoon but a fishing rod to battle Moby Dick.

READY ON THE RAILS

The reassuring cry from an American fly floor that those up there are ready, muscles flexed to take it out or bring it in.

REHEARSAL (a)

The period of time, always useful and some say vital to a production, when the company, their director and their author (if still alive) get the chance to work out what their production's really all about and how they are going to present it to the world.

A rehearsal's time scale is quite elastic and can last from one hour (show abandoned) to one year (show postponed). In between these two, though, plays can generally jog merrily along in rehearsal for three to four weeks and musicals for five or six.

It's only when you remind everybody that an audience will be paying to watch them in a week that reality starts to loom and the first preview is cancelled.

REHEARSAL CALLS

Come in two forms: Firstly, written notices announcing forthcoming rehearsals (they look more impressive if printed but that does not necessarily make them any more accurate); Secondly, they metamorphose into flesh-and-blood rehearsals with live actors, but only if the live actors have managed to read the calls properly.

REHEARSAL FLATS

Will sometimes be introduced into rehearsals on empty stages when walls are requested by the director.

They can be used to emphasise the strict confines of the set, the sheer claustrophobia of the theme, or simply as a last desperate ploy to prevent actors sidling off into the wings and into the pub.

REHEARSAL ROOMS

Are where the rehearsals take place. Until recently the criteria governing such rooms demanded that they should never be comfortable, always difficult to find, seldom well heated, generally dirty and without security, telephones or functioning toilets.

Sadly these conditions are increasingly under attack from recent Equity and H & S regulations.

I say sadly because, without these conditions to complain about, actors have time not only to bitch about the show and their parts but also to recognise and criticise missed calls, missed breaks and, though it pains me to say it, mismanagement.

RELIGION AND POLITICS

You must be strictly non-committal on both these subjects in the workplace.

A neutral attitude is essential and so, to avoid any offence, I recommend that the wearing of your Iron Cross with burka be restricted to the privacy of home and recreational haunts.

REP

Rep stands for Repertory Theatre. Keen-sighted readers will have noted that I have made few passing references to reps before, for the very good reason that there are few of them left or, for that matter, ever really were.

"Hang on," I hear some of you say. "What about all those old luvvies banging on in all their books about all their days in all those Reps all round the country?"

Well, you're right, but still technically wrong, because in an ideal theatre world, true repertory theatre is when a permanent company based in one theatre can, in theory, perform a different show on every night of their season.

"Economic madness!" you cry. "That's impossible."

Indeed Regional Reps could never afford the money for such turnarounds. Besides, they would soon have been in danger of making their regional audiences mentally giddy. Instead, depending on their budgets and locations, they opted for a number of shows to be each produced for a week, a fortnight or a month's run.

Great days and great experience for all involved but sadly now those that survive are continually struggling to do so. So, should you be offered the opportunity of a rep job, take one while they last.

REPETITEUR (a)

Is the posh French word for a rehearsal pianist for posh opera or ballet companies.

RESTING

In days gone by many an actor could be observed in the corner of saloon-bar snugs nursing a pint and inhaling deeply on their Capstan Full Strengths as they grappled with *The Times* crossword.

These sightings could occur at any time from 11am onwards, the time when London pubs opened and half an hour earlier if they were located outside the Metropolis. After all, this was the pattern of a normal working day in the profession. But if the same actors were to be discovered still in their snugs at 7.30pm, they were technically 'resting'.

Being between jobs then was never something to be ashamed of and that blunt question "Working?" would be proudly countered by "Resting, dear boy, between creative impulses."

These days no one under the age of eighty speaks thus. Furthermore, the absence of a proper job-seekers' allowance and the galloping interest in the price of stimulants means that our creative impulses are fully engaged in the pursuit of ancestry-tracing, bee-keeping, cocktail-shaking, dado-painting, emergency plumbing, fire-swallowing, gerbil-rearing, house-sitting, interior decorating, jail-breaking, knowledge-learning, lap-dancing, mystery shopping, ornamental gardening, personal training, quill-plucking, road-running, spread-betting, Tube-busking, undertaking, voice-coaching, window-cleaning, x-raying, yoghurt-making, zither-playing to have any, any time to rest.

RESTORATION LEVY

Not a jocular Jewish dramatist from the 1660s but a small charge sometimes added to the price of theatre tickets to aid the much-needed modernisation of old theatres, heartlessly listed in the past and so condemned until recently to decades of deliberate decay.

RETURNS (the)

These are the printed sheets produced and distributed by the box office each night which tell the monetary value of the house and the advance.

RETURNS QUEUE

When a show is selling out it becomes the show to see. So despite the 'Sold Out' sign proudly displayed on the box-office window or the 'House Full' board on the pavement, you will often find an optimistic queue of people waiting patiently to see if any patron's superfluous tickets might be returned to the box office and so be put on sale.

This does happen, as patrons are not allowed to sell their tickets themselves on the theatre premises. Such practice technically constitutes touting and is illegal under the terms of the theatre's licence. If this all sounds a bit straight-laced, the underlying reason for this rule is to prevent real ticket touts going about their business in the foyer and force them to stand outside in, hopefully, the rain, sleet or whatever else Aeolus can throw at them.

REVIEWS

Newspaper, television, radio and Internet reviews are essential for the public awareness of a production. Most show reviews are mostly mixed. Good ones gain awards and profits and prove your career masters wrong. Bad ones can be maliciously pernicious and so the breath of life for many of us. If yours are in the latter category do not despair. A truly appalling collection can guarantee immortality for your show and if they concentrate on your performance, all printed quotes can be improved no end by judicious cutting with a sharp pair of scissors.

REVOLVE (a)

Basically revolves. It is either incorporated in the floor of the set or is a permanent feature of a theatre and is used by designers to facilitate scene changes rather than to make the cast giddy.

RICHARD THE THIRD

The Bard's best villain has some cracking lines for a CSM's crisis moments.

"I am not in the giving vein today" always works when you are asked for a sub and have just spent the last of the float yourself.

"Have done thy charm, thou hateful withered hag" suffices when the wardrobe mistress has burnt a hole in your last presentable shirt.

And "Conscience is but a word that cowards use" is useful when some ghastly charity collector questions your genuine unconcern for Aid for Antelopes.

I would add "Off with his head" but nowadays you can only use this freely when touring parts of the Middle East.

RIGGERS

Are strong, silent men with heads for height who work at dead of night. They'll come in after on-stage rehearsals and do the most unusual things with chains and hoists to keep all that scenery floating serenely up above your head.

RIOTS

Have often swept through theatres but none have so far equalled the OP Riots of 1809. The initials in this instance stood for Old Price and the riots came about when the management of the newly rebuilt Theatre Royal Covent Garden tried to introduce a New Price or NP. The Theatre Royal Drury Lane had burnt down in that year leaving Covent Garden as the only theatre licenced to perform full plays. This monopoly tempted the actor and part owner of the theatre, John Kemble, to raise the ticket price. Rioting commenced on September 1st and mayhem and chaos continued for almost three months until Kemble backed down and gave a public apology on December 15th. A famous triumph for the low waged and due for a possible revival if West End ticket prices accelerate very much more.

ROSIN

This solid residue after distillation of oil of turpentine from crude turpentine is to be found in the wings wherever there's a dance show.

Like a dance belt it's an essential part of a dancer's equipment to stop them slipping on the stage.

Each night all of *Swan Lake* can be observed prancing in the rosin box – but for God's sake don't tell Bill Oddie.

ROSTRA

Is the plural of rostrum which is a platform of varied sizes used on stage to elevate shorter actors. It can be of rigid construction or so built to collapse and fold for ease of transport. It's probably best to let the actors know beforehand which type they'll be standing on.

ROUND (to get a)

Is when an audience spontaneously applauds an actor's entrance, the end of a particularly well-delivered speech or on an exit line.

It is sometimes occasionally heard at the conclusion of an appalling performance as a testament to the relief of the onlookers.

It has nothing to do with that other equally rare actor phenomenon, getting a round in.

ROYALTY (a)

A royalty is a payment to a member of a show's creative team or the Top Turn taken from the weekly net profit of a show. It can be a set payment or one that varies according to the weekly profit margin.

RUFF (mastering the)

Not only the obligatory neckwear for any authentic dark-gloomed Jacobean Tragedies needing some urgent white relief, but the correct if challenging obligatory accent for those upper-lower-upper-class girls eager to become 'actresses' and so escape their 'posh totty' doom.

The former is difficult to act in and the latter difficult to act with.

Lady Annarexia Thricemore-Mercie-Mellors may be delightful to look at (under artificial light) but no one acting opposite her, let alone listening to her, will have a clue as to what words she is pre-nanc-ing unless she has firmly mastered a Ruff accent.

Thankfully Elocution Lessons these days are readily available, as with everything else on most South East London estates.

Only then can she be universally understandable and claim her right to be challenging, raw and gritty with her splendid, if muddled opening line "Shit that shutting door."

RUN (a)

Is the length of time a particular production plays in a theatre from a day to a decade and then some.

RUN THROUGH (a)

Has no connection with swords unless you've just impaled Mercutio by ill luck or grand design.

Generally, when a show has been rehearsed in bits to such an extent that everyone knows their lines and is getting a little bored, it's time for a

Run Through. That sharpens everyone up, for it means that the show is acted in its entirety from start to finish.

Usually, a first Run Through is watched not only by the director, but also the producer, the playwright and all 'interested' parties.

A CSM knows instinctively that their interest has been maintained if all remain to watch the second act.

RUNNING ORDER

The running order is the correct sequence of scenes that together and sometimes remorselessly make up the whole of a play.

It is quite common to find little bits of paper pasted on to the back of flats with the running order written on them. This is to help all remember, for example, that the iceberg hits the *Titanic after* the dockside scene at Southampton.

RUNNING TIME (the)

Closely watched by all who read the show report (usually the DSM), the running time is the time each act of the show takes to play, plus the length of the interval.

Therefore this information can alert interested parties that yesterday's *Long Day's Journey Into Night* didn't come down till dawn and that pauses need be tightened.

RUSK

A biscuit favoured by babies, not to be confused with –

RUST

Which is an oxide that causes iron and steel and other metal structures to corrode, deteriorate and eventually collapse. Rust is a perfidious danger to the very fabric of theatres and for both performers and costumes in such shows as *The Iron Man* and *The Wizard of Oz*.

LA SCALA

S IS FOR:

SCALA (La)

There are certain theatres in certain cities so famous that they have no need of an exact address.

Should you need to send a note to someone at 'La Scala, Milan' it will reach them. Likewise *une lettre* to the 'Opera Garnier, Paris' and, of course, a postcard to our very own 'London Palladium'.

Of this trio, La Scala has the further distinction of being universally regarded as a theatre totally dedicated to Opera.

Every Diva of the Art aspires to play there. Some sadly wait in vain for the powers that be must be sure that they can fill the house. A reference to their pulling power, of course, rather than their size and weight.

SCARPERING THE LETTY

Is not a culinary term. Desperate times can call for desperate acts, though you should never describe yourself as a 'desperate act', if only out of respect for English grammar. You see, just occasionally on tour, lack of funds may oblige you to surreptitiously decamp from your digs or hotel. If you know in advance that you will have to do a bunk, or in theatrical terminology, scarper the letty, remember, on checking in, to demand a ground-floor bedroom at the front. That way you won't fall into a flowerbed and are nearer the freedom of the open road.

SCORE (a)

Is a musical part which sits on each musician's music stand and helps keep open their books and auto magazines.

SECOND HOME ALLOWANCE

Now here's a heading worth alone the cost of this book for those of you still bent on an acting or stage-management career, and the good news is that you don't even need to become a Member of Parliament.

Your second home allowance isn't actually called that. It's known as a Relocation Allowance and although it is only payable for thirteen weeks, it's a nice little extra earner.

To claim it, all you will need is an address more than 60 miles from London.

It is crucial that the measurements from your front door to Charing Cross are absolutely accurate, i.e. more than that mileage, if only by a foot.

You see, some economical producers have been known to personally check this out by walking the distance with a ruler.

So, if in any real doubt about the exact mileage, when asked where you live at your next audition or interview, always answer "In transit".

That gives you a further chance of getting the allowance. Transit Camper Vans are not just the domain of Down Unders parked up on the South Bank. They are often spotted, full of actors, resting on the kerb in Cambridge (60.7 miles), but never Oxford (58.9 miles).

SECURITY

It is a sad indictment of our world today that our profession could be a potential target for terrorists, both foreign and homegrown. So it's comforting to know that managements are acutely aware of their responsibilities and the need for vigilance is installed in all of us who may have cause to be front of house or loitering at the stage door.

Guidelines are issued and regularly updated and you should make yourself aware of them. For example, be on your guard should you see someone approaching who appears to be mumbling, sweating, looking anxious, and clutching something in their clenched fist.

But before you call for help, do make sure it isn't the producer. He may have just picked up the nightly return from the box office.

SET (the)

The set of a play indicates where the play is set.

This can range from a loose interpretation to complete realism depending on the set designer's state of mind and budget.

SET (to)

Means when a director or choreographer stops changing his mind and decides that a certain way of, say, walking the plank, has the definitive number of steps and ordains that it must not be changed. So, it's set, even if the actor points out that he's still a foot away from his fall.

SET PROPS (to)

This is a careful and time-consuming task performed by your stage-management team prior to curtain up to ensure that all the props on stage and in the wings are there and in their right position. It is important that you have a back-up to shield you from the actors' wrath when 'things go missing'.

So, it is always useful to have the vital evidence of a 'Prop Check Tick Sheet'. This, no matter what isn't set, should be fully ticked before every show.

SETTING LINE (the)

Is that imaginary line which runs across the stage directly above the house curtain and is so called because nothing should be set below it, be that furniture, flats or stiffly posed actors, unless the director wants them to be in full view of the audience when the curtain is in.

For that matter nothing should be straddled over it – not only are the tabs above but also the iron – so leave it clear unless you want to witness a rather blunt version of the guillotine in action.

SHARK'S TOOTH (a)

Nothing to do with the more masculine variety of lucky charm of the rabbit-foot nature, a shark's tooth is the best type of opaque gauze for a transformation effect.

SHORT RUNS

Are basically when shows don't. The shortest on Broadway is possibly the English import *Songbook*.

Its run, despite the presence in the cast of Jeff Goldblum, closed after the opening night, but it is equalled by at least a couple of West End productions. *Oscar Wilde: The Musical* lasted all of one night at the Shaw Theatre in 2004.

Although Mike Read's creation was described by the *Evening Standard* as "a musical of exquisite awfulness" I'm pleased to say that the playwright/composer is not one to be discouraged by mere critics. Amongst several other works, he has also musically reinterpreted Shaykspeer with his version of *A Midsummer Night's Dream*, entitled *Oh Puck*.

Another production that lasted one night (17 December 1953) was the dangerously titled *Thirteen for Dinner* at the Duke of York's Theatre.

However, all are beaten to the post by *The Intimate Revue*. This opened on 11 March 1930 at the Duchess Theatre. Intimate and the Duchess go hand in hand, but whoever designed it had got his theatres muddled. The length and laboriousness of the scene changes meant that half the audience had left by the interval. In desperation, seven scenes from Act 2 were ditched but to no avail. The show was abandoned before the final curtain.

SHOW REPORTS

Are written after every night's performance to let all interested parties know what has happened during the evening's entertainment. That nothing does is a tribute to the discretion of the writer, usually the DSM, who wishes to avoid any reference to the agony, the ecstasy and anything else the cast may have taken.

What is recorded sometimes with greater accuracy, apart from the running times, is the weather. After all, it has blighted British holidays since time began, so why not audience figures?

SIFFLEURS

The correct Variety expression for bird-impersonation acts. These artistes are regrettably not heard as much as they used to be, possibly because of urban noise pollution.

SIT

Should be a pretty straightforward word. After all, it's one of those used endlessly at Cruft's. Always use it before disciplining someone. That way, if they're in that position and take offence at your words they'll probably miss your throat.

SITZEPROBE

A term possibly borrowed from the lower *Deutsche*. It is said to originate from the Uber Opernhaus von Krackitz's ancient yet joyous tradition of innovatively bringing singers and orchestra together for a *mitsingen* or singalong before they are separated by the barrier of *der Orchestergraben*.

Not to be confused with a *Zitzeprobe* when, once a month, musicians are allowed to squeeze each other's spots.

SKIP

Not that cissy thing boxers do but a wicker basket in which you lay your props and costumes and less attractive companions.

Skips are very robust and can survive the roughest tour, unlike your props, costumes and less attractive companions. I met one recently which accommodated both Sarah Bernhardt and her wooden leg.

SLAP

An old-fashioned term for stage make-up and still used in Pantoland.

The rouge, powder and greasepaint would be 'slapped on' the face, both lovingly and often. Not to be confused with 'strapped on' which refers to wooden legs as above, or other things slightly higher up.

SLIP (a)

We all slip at times, but when you become a CSM – many, many, many times.

To maintain your dignity you have to understand that it's not your fault. The best intentions not to can be destroyed in seconds.

All it needs is the understudy to find out that, though he's about to go on, not one single member of the audience, with the sole exception of his mother or his lover, will ever know. Everyone else sitting out there will presume that the actor Chalfont St Just has had a cheap Romanian facelift or hasn't been able to afford new photos since 1979.

The next thing you'll know is that your office door will fly open and there will be the understudy demanding his Equity rights.

It's no good arguing about carbon footprints. Get busy on your computer. Print out a specimen slip for his mother or lover and hand it to him with a promise that hundreds more will be run off. As soon as he's gone, phone the box office. Find out the number of punters, divide by three and then print out the number required.

Guillotine them (see *Safety in the Workplace*) and hand deliver them, if you've any digits left, to the programme kiosk.

And, if the understudy has been really Bolshie, do remember to misspell his name and maybe more...

OWING TO THE SUDDEN INDISPOSITION
OF
Mr CHALFONT ST JUST

THE PRIVATE PART
OF
SILAS MAGGOT

WILL BE PLAYED WITH
BY
Miss JEREMY TOOTLE

SLOSH

Comes with Christmas for it is the white foam used to splosh over everybody in panto.

It can be sampled in Jack's Mother's Dairy in *Jack and the Beanstalk*, or in Sarah the Cook's Kitchen in *Dick Whittington* and for that matter in any interior scene where mayhem is needed.

According to Dorcas Wood – the Delia Smith of Slosh – to make it properly you will need:

One bucket
One shaving soap stick
One cheese grater
One whisk
Hot water in a separate jug sufficient to fill the bucket
and Half a bottle of glycerine per bucket

"Holding the shaving stick in one hand, grate it with the other and allow the particles to fall into the bucket. Next add the glycerine and whisk slowly while adding the hot water in an even steady flow and, having done this, you should have achieved 'perfect slosh'. However, never forget that the mixture will need to be re whisked just before it goes on stage to achieve perfect volume, sheen and flexibility."

Using this recipe means that the slosh is eye, hair and wardrobe friendly. So do not be ever tempted to use a substitute.

Finally, a word of caution: Good stage managers as a rule always lay in adequate supplies of props and effects to avoid running short over the dark days of Christmas. However, do not be tempted to buy up all the glycerine from the chemists of Colchester, or wherever you are playing in one fell swoop. That way you will avoid having to answer to the Special Branch or MI6, as glycerine is also an essential part of any self-respecting DIY bomb-maker's recipe.

SMA

These initials stand not for a criminal organisation as found in a James Bond novel, but for the Stage Management Association. This organisation helps its members find work by the distribution of a free list that appears each month, seemingly at the time of the full Moon. It is many, many pages long and contains the names of all those seeking employment with brief, if strangely similar, coded descriptions of their experience, aspirations and talents. It is very, very useful for those managements not of a nervous disposition.

SNAKE

This business is full of silver-tongued specimens sibilantly promising heaven and earth to the innocent amongst us. Beware these foul serpents or at least be aware of them.

You should also watch out for another variety of snake, equally deadly.

It is the name for a massed coil of sound-department cables. These foul obstacles have done more damage over the years to people's ankles than all that feedback has done to people's ears.

SOBOM

Is a shadowy organisation known as the Society of Box Office Managers.

Very little is known about SOBOM except that it holds a secretive Christmas lunch each year for its members and guests. No one is prepared to admit what actually happens then, but the fact that it has can be verified by the state of the Box Office Managers on the next day.

SOLT

Stands for the Society of London Theatre. This august body was founded by Sir Charles Wyndham in 1908 and to this day represents the vested interests of commercial producers and theatre owners. Unlike SALT it does not carry a Government Health Warning.

SOUND DEPARTMENT (the)

Many, from their own experience, regard this title as something of an oxymoron.

Sound is a fairly new addition to the world of theatre, if you recall that amplification only started in the 1920s.

I myself equate it to the Wild West. Here they are, the good guys, brilliant designers and fine operators struggling to keep the peace with their DPA 4061s and dedicated in the fight to clean up feedback. Meanwhile, all around them roam gangs of desperadoes and stick-on artists who can clip a Seinnheiser to anybody in seconds but don't know how to mix a desk without years of corrective training.

The wonder is that these cowboys call themselves sound engineers. However, before you too rush to apply for that job in *The Stage*, remember, you have to have a vital qualification to battery up, and that, of course, is to be slightly deaf.

SPANISH (the)

When, after an audition, an actor tells you he's had the Spanish, he is, of course, referring to the el bow.

SPEC ACT (a)

Is what thin-lipped, tight-teethed razor-blade-eaters call themselves, and although they may monopolise your first-aid box they are not alone.

Speciality acts are living proof of the limitless magnitude of human imagination and of our boundless ability to attempt the impossible. However, if you too want to become a spec act, first invest in a subscription to *The Lancet* in order to find out what cannot be digested or caught safely by any of your appendages.

SPEECH

The gift of speech should not be confused with the art of speaking. Most of us are granted the first, but only those of us lucky enough to enter the worlds of the stage, politics or religion can bore the rest of the world with the latter.

SPEED RUNS

Usually happen when there's nothing else to do on the afternoon of a first night.

These generally only take place for plays; on Musical first nights, there's usually a second act to compose, write, and rehearse. The play's director gathers the cast in the stalls and after extolling the advantages of artistic interpretive freedom, orders them to do a line run at double the speed of sound, omitting not so much as an 'and' from the author's text. The inevitable result is collective memory loss on page 39 and sore-tongue syndrome for the more delicate of players.

SPELLING

Should not be taken two seriously in this business. Actors being slightly self-centred, as long as you spell your cast names correctly on there dressing rhume doors you will get away with any other dereviations.

SPLIT WEEK (a)

Happens when a producer decides that his touring show should play two dates in one week. This does not often happen these days and doesn't at all if the truck breaks down somewhere between Aberdeen and Plymouth.

SPONTANEOUS COMBUSTION

Does happen and is more common in the world of Theatre than anywhere else. However, if many performances spontaneously combust it's usually on opening nights, or when casting directors are in. For the rest of the run they are inclined to implode.

SPOT A DEAD

Is not only something a lynx-eyed usher observes fifteen minutes after curtain down huddled in D13 of the Stalls. It is a term that also applies, with the same ophthalmic precision, to Master Carpenters or Production Managers when they, from the safety of the Stalls, give the definitive height for the dead of any masking material flown.

SPOTS

The individual, hand-guided lights that enhance and emphasise 'star' performances from entrance to exit. They are there just in case the audience haven't realised that they are privileged to be watching a star performance.

On the Spot is:

(a) a technical term for a technician who works a follow spot in between refreshment breaks.

(b) an old Edgar Wallace thriller set in the Chicago of the 1930s. Several famous actors have played Tony Porrelli, the professional mobster and amateur organist, including Charles Laughton and Simon Callow who also, of course, wrote Laughton's definitive biography.

SRO

Stands for Standing Room Only. These initials are muttered tersely from the corner of a Box Office Manager's mouth either when every seat in the house has been sold, or when every seat in the house has been sold off for scrap metal and is tonight on a slow boat to China.

ST PAUL'S, COVENT GARDEN

Is the Actors' Church. It was designed by Inigo Jones who created masques for Charles I and Henrietta Maria and, as it opened in 1633, predates Wren's Cathedral. It has been associated with the theatre since 1662. It was on 9 May of that year that Samuel Pepys wrote in his diary that he had seen an Italian puppet show performed under the church's portico. This is the first English mention of a Punch and Judy show. Since then an immense selection of actors, famous and obscure, have been associated with St Paul's, though none have outlived Mr Punch. Their commemorative plaques cover the church walls and though the graveyard can no longer accommodate thespian bones, the flowerbeds have been known to occasionally receive actors' ashes. This practice is not encouraged or for that matter allowed, so if your late old mate insists on being sprinkled there, first study a DVD of *The Wooden Horse* or *The Great Escape* and then have copies made of the sand-dispersal socks to place inside your trousers.

STAGE (the) (1)

The playing area on which actors perform in full view of their public.

STAGE (The) (2)

Long ago, when the question was posed as to what were the three most useless things in the world, the answer would invariably be the Pope's balls and a good review in *The Stage*.

But that was long ago. Nowadays our industry's newspaper is much more driven and hard-hitting, has gone tabloid and doesn't stain your fingers.

It comes from sustainable trees and can be used as a legitimate expense so it's our collective duty to support it. Go on. Stop reading someone else's. Buy your own copy.

STAGECRAFT

An actor enters too soon and so has nothing yet to say or do. He must make a quick decision. He can either (a) sit down and watch the others, or (b) exit quietly, mouthing 'sorry'.

If his choice is (a), he knows his stagecraft.

STAGE DIRECTIONS

Are, once a show's been blocked, the correct positions for an actor to be at, or by, on a specific line of dialogue. Often included with the text should the play be published, they can sometimes be misleading for the less experienced player. Stage Directions, therefore, should not be assumed. To illustrate this may I give an example:

Scene: A Dining Room
Actor One turns from DSC to deliver a line to Actor Two who at this point of the play should be USC of him, only to discover that his words are addressed to emptiness.

Frantically searching the room he eventually finds Actor Two crouched underneath the legs of the table. The scene resumes though some vital visual contact, of the eyeball-to-eyeball variety, is sadly lost.

When asked afterwards for an explanation for his behaviour, Actor Two whips out his French's Acting Edition and declares that he was only following the stage direction.

And there it is in black and white: 'Sit below table.'

STAGE LEFT

The area of stage to the left of the centre line.

STAGE RIGHT

The area of the stage to the right of the centre line.

STAGE SCREW

Is exactly what you think it is – a screw specifically for the stage. It is used to anchor braces to the floor rather than use stage weights which a Stage Manager should never lift alone.

The stage screw is endowed with an eye that can be used to help it to enter the tougher type of plank. Please note that you will find most stage floors already covered in holes so be careful to make a fresh incision and be careful where you tread.

STAGE WEIGHT

Is basically a weight for the stage, a rectangular piece of cast iron put to use backstage to anchor braces holding up flats to the deck without having to use a stage screw. They are invariably heavy so juggling stage weights is not encouraged by caring Master Carpenters.

STAGE WHISPER (a)

In any other business this would be called a deafening shout but one that is still meant to convey a discreet confidence. To be fair, many actors can achieve a different subtle modulation to their volume of speech while others cannot.

STAGGER THROUGH (a)

Happens when a show has been fully blocked and is the first time that the scenes and acts are run through in their correct order, from top to tail. Depending on the time of day and the state of both the actors and their performances, a stagger through can sometimes live up to its name.

STANDING SET (a)

Does exactly that as long as it has been cleated, nailed and screwed to within an inch of its two by fours.

In fact it should remain rigidly upright for the whole run of the production, for the one thing about a standing set is that, unlike the cast, it never changes (see *The Mousetrap*).

As the years roll by, standing sets often acquire a sticky miasmic patina on and about their flats and furniture.

This substance oozes from the fetid breath of countless audiences and actors. So, when working on a standing set, avoid this discharge by never leaning on the walls or sitting on the sofas.

STRIKE

You'll have to accept this very grim prospect. Strikes happen every night somewhere in this business.

What should a CSM do about them?

Shut the Company Office door firmly. Bar or lock it. Walk straight out of the Stage Door and go directly to the pub. Don't worry. You won't be alone for long. Soon the other departments will have finished their strike, taken everything that belongs to the show and anything decent they've found in the theatre (see *Bar Snacks/Furniture /Usherettes*), be fully packed up and ready to join you for a fond farewell to whichever ghastly date you've been playing.

SUPER (a)

Is a supernumerary, the theatrical term for an extra with no lines to speak. Supers are found mainly in opera productions which require large crowd scenes. They are not found too often in plays these days as no say does not equate with no pay.

SUPERSTITIONS

Many of us in this business are, as Stevie Wonder observed, very superstitious, even if we do not necessarily wash our face and hands.

Theatrical superstitions are rooted in the knowledge that things can, and do, go horribly wrong on stage if the gods are angered...

I'd expand on this if I could, but I can't. I've been locked out of my dressing room and computer and all because I whistled the briefest snatch of Verdi's *Macbeth* and told the cast what it was...

SWAZZLE (a)

If you weary of working with others, have a penchant for violence and would like to become a professor you'll need one of these so that you can intone "That's the way to do it" as your colleague Mr Punch dispatches yet another victim.

SWEARING

It is not a good idea to swear at your fellow workers unless and until they are all swearing at you. You can then claim provocation but, of course, you must remember that they'll be doing the same.

Therefore keep profanities and vulgarisms to the minimum. Instead use certain innocuous words which will give you great inner pleasure. For example, calling someone a 'Berk' won't cause offence, for few theatre people are followers of horse and hound and fewer still ride with the Berkeley.

SWINGS

The sad thing about swings is that they don't have much time to. They are far, far too busy, poring over charts and diagrams and learning all the steps and moves and words and music of all those in the musical ensemble they're allocated to understudy. The end result is that those they cover can swing to their hearts content in the sure knowledge that when they phone in sick, it's the swings who'll cover.

SWORD SWALLOWING

Is not for beginners or for those suffering from displaced necks. Having once attempted to learn this ancient theatrical art I can only say (with some difficulty) that one should never start with a scimitar.

TABS

T IS FOR

TABS (the)

Are the house curtains, usually made from heavy red or blue velvet and generally as old as the theatres in which they hang. Don't get caught underneath them when they come in or you'll have to be sent to the dry cleaners.

TAB TRACK (a)

Not your bar bill at Gerry's but a flown track for hanging and operating the tabs.

TAB WARMERS

Is the name for an FOH lighting state plotted into the LX board so as to give vibrant life and extra colour to those old tabs above.

TACHOGRAPHS (digital)

I suppose it was inevitable. Following the introduction of the 'Working Time Directive', EU regulators are at this moment arguing over legislation that may make it compulsory for all technicians to wear a personal tachograph.

These sinister ankle contraptions have been developed in a joint venture by the Hildebrand Institute, Bad Mannheim, Germany, and Laboratoire Temperdu, Arrêt le Cloche, France.

Their aim is accurate and binding and, having been involved in a trial wearing, I can warn you all that they can make you limp. However, all is not lost. Given our national quest for getting legless I can't see many of our industry's workers being able to get them on.

TANTRUMS
(see *Hissie Fits*)

TAP

A tap routine, which involves no plumbers but at least one dancer, can enhance the dreariest show. Purists will advocate Musicals; desperadoes, Galsworthy.

TAX

It's a sad fact of life that two things are inevitable: Death and Income Tax.

You'll never escape the former but those of you who find work as actors or stage managers will be able to avoid the latter at least until the end of each year.

There's one golden rule for all of you who are thus technically self-employed: Keep your receipts and anyone else's you can lay your hands on.

TAXI

As a vital cog in the theatrical machine, one needs to take an overall view of one's indispensability.

This doesn't take long but the safest way to arrive there is by taxi.

And please get a receipt (see *Tax*).

TAXIDERMISTS

You're going to be told to "Get stuffed" many times throughout your career.

You shouldn't take it to heart but, just in case, keep a list of local taxidermists about your person. Hand it to your tormentors with the proviso that they pick up the bill.

TEASER (a)

There's nothing like a teaser to raise some people's blood pressure and set their pulses racing. If that is the case in this case, then you're working with those who are unnaturally stimulated by black serge. A teaser is nothing more (though you must never upset them by telling them so) than a border set behind the proscenium whose drop is brushed by a tormentor on either wing to complete an inner masking frame.

Do you know something? I find that quite appealing, in the visual sense, of course.

TECHIES
(see *Crew*)

TECHNICAL DRESS REHEARSAL

Before a Dress Rehearsal it is customary and advisable to have a Technical Dress Rehearsal which on occasions can seem to take longer than the entire rehearsal period put together. This is because all the complex technical cues have to be worked through from beginning to end, for very often this is the first time that they have been run in sequence.

This can cause endless delay when the need to ring the doorbell before the door opens is discovered and rectified.

TELEPHONES (on stage)

Many stage-plays still incorporate telephones as plot essential props. The drawback is that directors always want them to ring. My advice is to let the Sound department deal with this demand. Should you be on the book and miscue the ring, always insist it rang. Massed mobile phones in the auditorium and blanket tinnitus on stage should cover you completely. Conversely, should you be acting on stage when it miss rings, pick it up. You then have the choice of two lines. "It's a wrong number" will usually get a sympathy laugh but, "It's for you" as you hand the telephone towards another actor is much more fun.

TEMPO

Is the speed at which the Musical Director conducts but not necessarily what the orchestra play.

TERPSICHORE

Was one of those nine Muses who razzle dazzled the ancient world with a pretty unbeatable act. She and her sisters Calliope, Clio, Euterpe, Thalia, Melpomene, Erato, Polyhymnia and Urania, were the daughters of Zeus and Mnemosyne and their routine encompassed all the arts.

From her name comes the word 'terpsichorean' meaning 'of or relating to the dance', for Terpsichore, lyre in one hand, Apollo in the other, was renowned as a bit of a mover, in fact the Muse of the Dance.

THEATR

Is correct in Mold, Wales, but must be treated as a misspelling when found on barn doors in Bratislava.

THEATRE

Is the English way of spelling the word. Theater is the American variation.

Both are right but only in their specific countries.

THEATRE OF THE ABSURD (the)

It would be tempting, I am sure, at times to reply, "When was it ever not?" However, this is a perfectly genuine genre typified by the plays of Beckett (Samuel), Ionesco (Eugene) and Simpson (N.F.).

THERE'S NO BUSINESS IN SHOW BUSINESS

Is the desperate cry heard on a wet Saturday in Wigan when the producers of *Annie Get Your Gun* get sight of the weekly figures.

THESPIAN

Is another name for an actor and one that once again goes back to Ancient Greece. Thespis of Attica won first prize in the first Let's Be Tragic contest in Athens in around the year 534 BC. The term was widely used in the Victorian era when the business was trying to become respectable, but its use did not necessarily make the acting any better.

THRUST STAGE (a)

Is one that sticks out into the auditorium; another name for an apron stage.

THUD AND BLUNDER

Is, of course, not only a Spoonerism, but a perfect description for a Get In or Out after a good, long lunch or dinner hour.

TIDGE IT IN/OUT

A technical command used when asking for a flying piece to be lowered in or raised out inch by inch with the most delicate precision. The visual result can be almost imperceptible – until it crashes into the deck or grid.

TIE

Stands for Theatre in Education. Having bought this book you have reversed the experience.

TIGHT

Singular of...

TIGHTS

Unless you're a woman or have to walk on in a T.I.E. tour of Shakespeare it is advisable never to wear tights at work. They are bound to ladder.

TIMESHEETS

Otherwise known as Great Works of Fiction. These go to prove how much hidden talent lies dormant until Saturdays in this industry.

If you're pressed to sign them, three words of good advice: Illegibility, Illegibility, Illegibility.

TIMING

It's all in the timing, as any actor will tell you. In fact this whole business is about timing. The most unlikely success is a success because it is exactly what people want to see at the time. Revive it five years later and it dies a death. Good timing from an actor can extend a smile at an exit line into a huge laugh and roars of applause.

Bad timing can make him leave the set in silence but he'll soon make up for it.

Observe him after the show, having been bought a pint, regaling the room with a story long enough to last until it's his round. He drains his drink, puts his hand in his pocket, pulls out a tenner, drops it on the floor and is still crawling in pursuit when the bell goes, the lights come up and closing time is called.

TOBACCO

Is now publicly frowned upon by practically every authority under the sun, though the pension industry has a generous attitude to those who inhale.

Actors can still smoke on stage but it has to be because of significance – Musicals such as *The Man in the Iron Lung* – or an historic association with a character played: Popeye, Sherlock Holmes or Winston Churchill.

TONIC (a)

Is the perfect companion to a Vera.

TONY (a)

Broadway's top award for actors, the equivalent of our Oliviers, has been handed out since 1947. It is actually named the Antoinette Perry Award to honour the American actor and director who was also instrumental in the creation of the Stage Door Canteens during the Second World War.

TOP

'From the top' is an expression meaning from the start of the show or scene.

It is used by mainly over-the-top directors.

TOP TURNS

Are your Stars, though this term is more common in Musical Theatre; however, Straight Theatre Stars can turn too, at the drop of a line.

TORCH (a)

Is a very useful aid backstage as it does get rather dark in the wings.

The choice of professionals is a Maglite. They come in all sizes so be sure to borrow one light enough not to sprain your wrist.

TORMENTORS (the)

Are not difficult directors but a pair of narrow black-felt flats placed directly behind the proscenium to reduce stage width when required.

TOSCA

Giacomo Puccini's (see *Name Dropping*) great opera and one which keeps popping up for you to work on because there are only three principal parts; not for yourself, of course, but for three glass-breaking voices, Cavaradossi, Scarpia and yes, you've got it, Tosca.

That's why it's never too hard to cast, even at short notice for the Sleaford Operatic Society. However, there are two elements to it that can make it all go tits up (see *Mattress/Firearms*).

TOURETTE (or not Tourette)

Years ago it was very simple. If someone stood up in the Stalls and shouted and swore at the actors it was obviously the director. Nowadays modern advances in analytical medicine have clouded our certainty. The fat lady screaming obscenities at today's matinee could be the director in drag but an equal possibility is that it's a Care in The Community out and up for a rare cultural treat.

TRAD

Stands for Thespian Related Adjustment Disorder. Don't despair; if you feel you may be becoming a victim of this widespread though little talked about condition, you're in the right job. This sudden, sinister condition can strike faster than a DBO (see *DBO*) and can be great fun.

My late friend Graham Locknee would sometimes saunter into foyers with a cheery "Good Morning, Gorgeous" and the next moment start viscously assaulting the nearest display board and theatre manager.

This would happen, of course, only if some irresponsible member of the company had substituted 'jaw' for 'knee' on the cast board.

TRADITIONS

Are sometimes mistakenly linked with superstitions (see *Never Wear Goatees*). Traditions are rather codes of ancient theatrical behaviour and are always prefixed by *Never* and *Always*. For example: Never enter a theatre through the FOH if you're working there, and: Always exit through the FOH to avoid those other menacing traditions, underage fans, angry husbands, distraught wives et cetera.

TRANSFORMATION (a)

Is when a set of scenery moves and another takes its place before the audience's very eyes. This can involve flying and automation and all manner of cunning equipment so it is best to stand back and admire it all and let those that 'know' get on with it.

TRAPS

Traps are an ancient theatrical device, used since the days of Roman Theatre for dramatic entrances and exits through the floor of the stage.

There are several types of traps, usually worked by counterweights. They include the Grave Trap for *Hamlet*, the Cauldron Trap for *Macbeth* and the Von Trapp for *The Sound of Music*.

A 'Star' Trap is befittingly far more exciting if far more dangerous. It's a circular trap and when the lower half of its solid floor cover is dropped or slid back, the Star can burst through the upper-hinged segments. The solid cover is then immediately reinstated. Please note that this one really does rely on timing being everything.

Lastly, remember you must never, no matter how impatient, force the Hymen Trap for *As You Like It*.

TRAVELLERS

One of the many things you must not be in this business is prejudiced. You may well have to work far away from home in places where you will encounter travellers.

You can blame the town hall if you like, but for many years councils have baulked at spending public money just to build a flytower over their municipal stages in order to allow a minority Art the easy luxury of flying out the house tabs. Travellers are perfectly acceptable to an audience. They can be swagged. They part in the middle so they can even be paged and the only drawback is that you will have to work them fully dressed to avoid embarrassment or suggestions from all the rest of the crew on the deck.

TRAVOLATOR (a)

Is a moving belt of rubber that is set horizontally on the stage to move vertical actors across from one side to the other. They will remain vertical as long as the temptation to go for 'Full Speed Ahead' is resisted.

TREADS

Are sets of solidly built wooden steps of varying length for shorter actors to mount rostra, ponies and performances. A single tread is the domain of the taller actor.

TRIPE

Is either what the audience think of your show or, more comfortingly, what you will dine on afterwards. May I recommend Tripes à la Mode de Caen:

At least a pound of tripe (for two)
An ox hoof

Three large onions
Four carrots
A *bouquet garni*
Four leeks
A litre of cider
Half a bottle of Calvados
Salt, pepper, cloves and a sharp knife.

Soak in water, boil, clean, wash, wash and wash the tripe until you can look at it without feeling queasy. Cut it into chunks. Salt and pepper. Remove the bones from the hoof. Wash, wash, wash et cetera.

Put the bones, carrots, onions, leeks and the *bouquet garni* into a deep pot, place the tripe on top of them and then add the hoof. Pour in the cider and the Calvados.

Bring to the boil. Cover the pot tightly and bake it in the oven for eight hours at a low steady heat.

Remove carefully, eat lovingly but please remember – it's only tripe.

TRUSS

A hidden part of many an old actor's armoury. A strictly personal aid and not one supplied by the management.

TRUST

Another overworked word in the business. Always mentally insert a silent 'Never', whenever you hear it.

TUMBLER (a)

Was a type of vaudeville/variety acrobat whose speciality was, conveniently, tumbling. With somersaults no longer being the draw they used to be, this act is not often encountered professionally these days. However, I am glad to say that the practice still carries on at an amateur level at theatre parties, even if the outcome is invariably A & E.

TURNS
(see *Twirlies*)

214

TWIRLIES

You may have guessed already but twirlies are indeed the ladies and gentlemen of a Musical's ensemble.

They are fundamentally different from their near relatives, the turns, for that species, being actors in a Musical, speak clearly and move their legs to the left and right though seldom at the same time.

Twirlies, by comparison, are capable of completing full circles of the stage whilst executing graceful arm and leg movements at the same time. They sing loudly to the top of, and above, their vocal range.

In these dark days of austerity and funding cuts, large ensembles are on the decrease. Managements are always tempted to make savings but artistic standards must be retained and technically an authentic ensemble must contain, in order to retain its name, at least two twirlies.

So grab a ticket now for your nearest Musical before one twirlie goes off sick, the other on holiday and the swing cover becomes a featured solo.

TWOFERS

Are nothing more than two tickets for the price of one, unless you're watching a late-night cable television channel.

Twofer offers are sometimes printed on tiny bits of paper but this doesn't mean that you will have to share your seats with six other hobbits.

Please remember that to get best value for this offer, you will always have to take someone with you, unless you wish to sprawl horizontally over the armrest between seats. This practice is still not an illegal offence.

UBU ROI

U IS FOR:

UBU ROI

Alfred Jarry's play created a sensation at its première in 1896. King Ubu's first word "Merdre!" (Shitr) stopped the show in its tracks for a quarter of an hour while half the audience booed and the other half cheered. It still challenges to this day and is considered the forerunner of the Theatre of the Absurd.

UKULELE

Is a small Hawaiian member of the guitar family. Ever since George Formby held his in his hand its popularity in the UK has never ceased. Even played with fatuous abandon by Bertie Wooster, the flag now is flown by the magnificent Ukulele Orchestra of Great Britain who, as they say, treat the audience to "one plucking thing after another."

ULCER (an)

Not something YOU should ever suffer from.
   An ulcer should strictly be what you give other people.

UNDERDRESSING

If, during a show, you come across a member of the company who appears to be suddenly grossly overweight, do not immediately attempt to administer lymphatic drainage.
   You should first enquire whether he or she is practising the ancient, hidden art of underdressing. This takes place when an actor puts one or several costumes under the one they will first appear in. The logic behind this is that once its scene is over, it can be whipped off without the actor having to go back to the dressing room. It could also be because the central heating has broken down.
   The art of underdressing is to put the costumes on in the right order so that the last change required is next to semi-naked flesh. This does not always quite work out as it should.

Lastly, should you see a pair of flared jeans underneath Lady Bracknell's morning gown it has nothing to do with a new interpretation of the final scene.

It is merely that Lady B.'s cab has turned up early at the stage door and the clock's ticking over.

UNDERSCORE (an)

Is when music is played under dialogue in a Musical. This is so as to heighten dramatic intensity or to try to hide mundane inanities.

UNDERSTUDIES

Or covers, as they are more generally titled today, are actors engaged to cover other actors' parts. Some, with nimble dexterity, play their own parts as well, and then step up or into their colleagues' roles when the need arises. Others, however, spend their shows moving restlessly between the wings and their dressing rooms and are so known as 'walking' understudies.

The rule of thumb is that one understudy covers never more than two or three parts.

This is to avoid the more sensitive members of the cast from having nervous breakdowns when having to cope with too many identical interpretations from the said understudy.

UNDERTAKERS

Whether on tour or in town, it's always good to have an up-to-date undertaker's brochure open on your desk. The price list of their services will quietly help restore the more desperately sick in your company to rude good health.

UNDERWEAR

An actor is not allowed to don another actor's underwear if it is provided by the management. This rule applies till curtain down.

UNICORN (the)

Throughout its history Theatre has spawned many a legend, both glorious and monstrous. The bad ones usually get the best press, so to help right the balance it's only fitting that mention should be made of the Unicorn.

Named after that mythical beast which only believers can see, Caryl Jenner founded her children's theatre company in 1947 and it continues to this day to delight young audiences at its current home in Tooley Street.

UNION (the)

Is that powerful organisation that controls and rules all things technical backstage in America.

UNMENTIONABLE (the)

Is, dare I mention it, *Macbeth*. This, though the shortest of the Bard's tragedies, has had an ill reputation for longer than any other play in theatrical history.

Trouble started on its first performance, which some claim to have been on 7 August 1606, at Hampton Court in the presence of King James I.

We are told that Hal Berridge, the boy actor playing Lady Macbeth, did become feverish and died. His death was the start of a catalogue of disasters and accidents that have marred productions ever since.

The list of leading actors hurt is impressive and includes Mrs Siddons, Sybil Thorndike, Orson Welles and Charlton Heston, whose tights caught on fire.

The set collapsed at a dress rehearsal at the Royal Court in 1928 seriously injuring many; Olivier just missed being flattened by a falling counterweight in 1937; and a production in 1942 witnessed the deaths of two Witches and a Duncan and the suicide of the set designer.

Some accidents are self-inflicted. Diane Wynyard chose to play the sleepwalking scene with her eyes closed and fell predictably fifteen feet into the pit.

Others are inflicted. Many an actor has been run through in the battle scenes and one, Harold Norman, was killed by a sword thrust at the Oldham Coliseum in 1947.

One logical reason given for all these misfortunes is that, as the play is mostly set at night, poor lighting is to blame. However, actors, being superstitious, have learnt that it's best to respect the dim unknown. They refer to it as 'The Scottish Play', for the title itself, if spoken, brings ill luck. Should it be said, the culprit must leave the dressing room, turn around three times, spit, swear, knock thrice on the door and beg to be admitted.

I myself have seen... I'm sorry. I must conclude this section. My pencil has just stabbed me violently and snapped in half.

UP

When you are asked what time you go up, it's nothing personal, merely a question as to what time your show starts. This also applies to what time do you come down?

UPPER CIRCLE (the)

Is high above the Dress Circle, a hinterland where directors and producers seldom venture. After all, why should they exhaust their legs to climb so far when their focus is on those who've paid for the best? But is that for the best seats or the best performances? Trips to the Upper Circle can be quite illuminating.

UPSTAGE

Is the area of the stage furthest from the audience.

UPSTAGING

On those rare occasions when an actor feels he could contribute more to a scene and help the audience better appreciate his role, other members of the cast may find that instead of being parallel with them for their next bit of dialogue, he has moved ever so slightly upstage and they will have to turn their backs to the audience to engage in eyeball to eyeball conversation. It's rude and sometimes dangerous to turn your back on an audience so should you observe the whole company leaning nonchalantly on the back wall of the set you know that the original upstager is in a checkmate situation.

That is unless he exits the set and plays the rest of the scene from outside the French window.

URANUS

Is going to pop up now and then in conversation so when it's time to be serious you can say that: Uranus is actually the seventh planet from the Sun and was first discovered in 1781 by William Herschel with the aid of his telescope. It is named after the Greek God of the skies. And yes, it does have rings.

URGENT

Nothing is that urgent unless you've sent it to yourself.

URIAH HEEP

Potential Stage Managers have a lifestyle choice when it comes to this name.

They can, if they so wish, emulate the Dickens character in carving a career.

After all, a little obsequiousness and a good dose of insincerity can go a long way in this business.

However, they might wish to behave a bit more like the rock group of the same name. More fun, but please remember that that particular five-man band has had at least twenty-four different members since its conception.

USHER

To clear things up, you may officiate as an usher at a wedding or a funeral, but never as an usher at a theatre unless you can wangle a posting to the Upper Circle away from knowing eyes.

UV LIGHTING

Shouldn't be confused with Strobe Lighting. The latter can bring on epileptic fits while UV lighting is used in nightclubs and is deep purple which takes us back to – Uriah Heep.

VALMOUTH

V IS FOR:

VALMOUTH

Not the first deep-water port in Cornwall, but a witty musical by Sandy Wilson. Worth mentioning if someone's rabbiting on about *The Boy Friend* being the only thing he's ever composed.

VANYA

Is the diminutive of the Slavic name Ivan, meaning 'God is gracious'.

The most famous of all the many Vanyas is Uncle, who is the eponymous character of Anton Chekhov's famous play, first seen at the at the Moscow Art Theatre in 1899 when directed by Constantin Stanislavski.

Vanya is also used as a female name in Sweden and Bulgaria so must not be confused with the former if you should ever come across *Auntie Vanya*. This tragic, if little known play from Vastra Gotaland, concerns rivalries at a reindeer-eating competition. A production was recently advertised in Varna but was abandoned when the props were condemned as inedible.

VARIETY

The successors to the Music Halls, Variety shows were entertainments comprising of singing, dancing, juggling, acrobatic, novelty and comedy acts. The variety for the most part was in the sheer number of acts rather than in their individual variety, though real talent usually did out and speed off and away into theatre, radio, television and films.

VARILIGHTS

Are 'intelligent' lights which can change positions, colours and patterned gobos at the push of a button. This involves no wobbly ladder work. The button can be pressed from the LX desk by the wobbliest of fingers.

VENT

Is, for us insiders, the abbreviation for Ventriloquist, and not the slash in the back of our jackets. Ventriloquists are of another world so you're bound to get on with them.

However, a word of warning. Over the years, I have learned from bitter experience to stay well clear of them should they sidle over to me in the hotel after the show. I would advise you to do the same and thus avoid both crippling and baffling bar bills.

VERA (a)

Is, of course, rhyming slang for – a gin.

VERSE

Is when lines rhyme. Not advisable on shows less than three hundred years old unless sung through with a large band, but even then critics may still say the verse is yet to come.

VERTIGO

All of us can suffer from a recurring touch of the above and you should make clear at the very start of each engagement that you are a victim of this psychological phobia.

This will prevent you having to climb ladders on stage or flights of stairs to 'awkward' dressing rooms.

VET (to)

Working with some selfish actors, or animals as they are known, is one of the many hazards of this business, especially when you come in as a takeover and they just won't take to you. Sometimes they are not even housetrained and, if that's the case, it's no good hoping they'll change. Long runs, short runs, it's all the same to them. It will wear you down, so, if you really can't take any more, when no one's watching surreptitiously hit them hard around the head with a blunt prop.

Violence in the workplace is usually reciprocated but it's worth a stitch or two on your leg and a quick anti-rabies jab in the stomach to see

Lassie, or whatever the bloody dog's called, being taken away for a 'final' visit to the dispensary. Just make sure that you have a chance to vet its replacement.

VICTORIA (Queen)

Royalty has long patronised the Theatre. Regal enthusiasm can be robust, witness Charles II's appreciation for Nell Gwynne or Edward VII's for Lily Langtry but many are unaware that Queen Victoria was as besotted as any *Phantom* fan. Between 1837 and 1861 she attended more than 800 performances, taking in ballet and opera, Shakespeare, Sheridan, melodrama and comedy and, most favourably, the animal trainer Van Amburgh and his lions at Drury Lane.

The Royal Box may have gathered dust after Prince Albert's demise at many London theatres but by 1881 she was commanding performances again at Windsor and other Royal residences from the likes of Sarah Bernhardt, Beerbohm Tree and Henry Irving. Her enthusiasm for drama assisted Irving in gaining the first theatrical knighthood thereby making the former pastime of rogues and vagabonds a proper profession, though one, of course, still full of rogues and vagabonds.

VIP

Stands for Very Important Person. VIPs are really very common in the world of Theatre as everybody in it is a VIP – or so they tell their Mums.

VIPERIDAE

Animal Rights will now probably stop you from using a live snake on stage in *Antony and Cleopatra*, but it's useful to know that an *Aspis* was a symbol of royalty in Egypt and its bite, though lethal, is, to this day, fairly painless.

VIRTUE

In a business that relies on regular doses of sordid immorality to ensure headlines, employment and success, it is hard for anybody to know which of the virtues they should try to pursue to retain some moral ground.

I would suggest to you that the best option is to go for *Virtue in Danger*, courtesy of Sir John Vanbrugh.

VISION

Another directorial word used often at read throughs, as in "the authors' vision of today will be explained tomorrow". This means, of course, that everyone, including the authors, are still in the dark.

VISIONS

Creative teams sometimes have sudden visions as to how a production should look.

Technicians have daily visions of how it does.

VITRIOL

Sheer venom. Sometimes encountered in the workplace.

VIXEN

Should your lead tenor say they're doing *The Cunning Little Vixen* they are not referring to that member of the ensemble who has lost her principles and is working her way through them; he means Janacek's opera which is always on somewhere to help prove the point that Opera is not just Italian, German, Russian or French.

VODKA

Vodka should always be drunk chilled and neat. If you add tonic you've got a drink problem.

VOICE (the)

Is really rather vital in this business unless you're circus-based. You must make sure your artistes look after theirs. Many things are bad for the *voce* including those everyday props of the profession, fags and drink. Preventive therapy, rather than visits to those dark rooms in Harley Street when things have gone too far, is becoming increasingly popular with singers. This takes the now fashionable form of throat massages.

This hands-on throat contact really seems to help but CSMs, however tempted, shouldn't have a go unless really, truly provoked.

VOLCANOES

Can erupt all over the theatre but most often in your Top Turn's dressing room. One minute you're talking quietly about the performance and the next they're exploding about someone else's.

Never agree. Never disagree. Call for the Resident Director – if the Top Turn's still talking to them.

VOLE

Often mistaken for a small mouse, voles frequently overrun many an isolated, rural theatre. However, you won't see many of these fierce, nocturnal creatures as most isolated, rural theatres are closed at night.

VOMIT

Sadly happens on the best of shows. If your turn looks like they might, a bucket in either wing is just the thing. If set with ostentatious ceremony and loud explanation it may even help to avoid that technicolour yawn.

VORTEX (the)

Is a very old play by the then very young Noël Coward.

It's all about sex and booze and drugs and still works today, proving that, yet again, nothing really changes.

WAGES

W IS FOR:

WAGES

Not exclusively a theatrical happening, but one which does occur in the profession, for contrary to some actors' stories, people actually *do* get paid from time to time.

It was said that the wages of Sin were Death, but then in 1483 one Robert Brown, a Yorkshire actor, demanded and received sixpence for playing the part of God in the play *Noah at Hull*.* His interpretation failed to bring down any divine displeasure and ever since then turns have been financially rewarded for their efforts though many will say, "only God knows why".

*To elaborate: The play *Noah* was merely performed at Hull. There is no evidence that Noah or his Ark ever docked there, despite the recent discovery of some fossilised giraffe dung in the University Library.

WALK DOWN (a)

Used to be a final moment of great theatrical ingenuity, but nowadays is more likely to be what happens at the end of a Musical when there's been no time to rehearse a choreographed curtain call or if no one has the skill to invent one.

WALK THROUGH (1)

Is something you have to be on constant guard against. It is the sordid practice of allowing people to view a show without so much as a ticket. Only a renegade member of this profession would tolerate such degenerate deviousness. You must not succumb.

WALK THROUGH (2)

If an actor is said to be walking through his part it means that he is giving a lacklustre and lifeless performance. The problem is compounded in many cases by a lifeless audience and a lacklustre play.

WALTER PLINGE

Was at one time one of the country's most versatile and much-in-demand actors. His name would appear in the cast list of programmes throughout the country, sometimes in several productions on the same night. This supernatural ability to be both at Windsor and Worcester at curtain up was because Walter was either playing an unseen character, pivotal to the plot, or because an actor, such as the late, great Warrington Minge, would insist on taking on this persona and nom de stage when playing a second footman or bootblack rather than risk ruining his reputation as an interpreter of a huge range of noble, if identical, upstairs characters.

WARBURTON'S COOK

Betsy Baker has a lot to answer for but, for that matter, so does John Warburton.

The former was the latter's cook and he himself was an early 18th-century antiquarian book collector as well as being the Somerset Herald.

Mr Warburton assiduously hunted down original rare manuscript copies of Elizabethan and Jacobean playwrights until his collection numbered some fifty or sixty plays. They included: *Henry I* by Shakespeer and Davenport; *Duke Humphrey* by Shekaspyre; *Cardenio* by Shakespear and Fletcher; *The Mayden Holady* by Marlowe; and many others by Massinger, Ford, Middleton, Dekker and Tourner .

For safekeeping he handed over this priceless collection to Betsy his cook but she in turn, in the interests of home economics, put their pages to different uses: "burnt or put under pie bottoms".

Betsy baked and Warburton, unknowingly and steadily, munched his way through his treasures until all but three plays had been devoured.

WARDROBE (the)

Is from where all the costumes for a show – deloused, laundered, stitched and starched – issue forth before the Half on their journeys to their dressing rooms.

It's a place of mystery and legend because, as it's always situated on the top floor, only a brave few have the stamina to mount those endless stairs and wake the sleeping beauty slumbering over the cobwebbed ironing board.

230

WARDROBE MASTER

I suppose beauty is not an essential qualification for a Wardrobe Master though it does help if you're a Wardrobe Mistress.

When first entering an industry so reliant on fantasy, some may imagine Wardrobe Masters to be tall bearded figures clad in flowing robes while grasping a well used iron. Wrong.

Others, when they think of a Wardrobe Mistress, picture her basqued and booted beating the life out of some sewing-machine. Wrong.

Instead, picture this: A tired veteran of either sex crouches over an ill-lit table wearily stitching together a moving mass of multi-coloured feathers. Wrong Again. Feather boas are bought made-up these days.

WARM UP (a)

Takes place in Musicals before the Half so that the company can literally warm up their muscles.

Muscles are not solely restricted to those that jauntily poke out from leg or arm or ripple on the stomach. They also lurk inside the mouth and so are known to those who are in the know as vocal muscles.

WATER

It is a stipulation nowadays that drinking water be provided for the cast. It is never advisable to drink theatre tap water. Therefore make use of your 'hernia' and so avoid lifting any of the huge bottles you will have to order to satisfy the universal thirst.

WATERFALLS

Should be discouraged on stage.

They are wet, warm and often breed mosquitoes.

WEATHER (the)

Is one important, if overlooked, factor that can determine a show's fortunes.

If it's snowing you'll lose audiences

If it's foggy you'll lose audiences
If it's raining you'll lose audiences
If it's sunny you'll lose audiences
And if it's a heat wave you'll lose your cast.

WEEE

Not an incontinent misspelling but the acronym for Waste Electical and Electronic Equipment – a directive that became European Law in 2003.

WEEK OUT (a)

Shows on tour sometimes do not play every week on the road due to the unavailability of suitable venues. When this happens it is called a Week Out and is taken by the cast as a holiday week or as an unpaid week depending on the generosity of the management.

WEEKLY (the)

Is one of Theatre's most important written documents, for it is the printed summary of the past week's takings at the box office.

WE'LL LET YOU KNOW

The audition phrase that is the theatrical equivalent of the death sentence.
    Remember to use downward inflections for heightened effect.

WHAT'SONSTAGE.COM

Is one of the very best theatre websites, informative and up-to-the-minute and one which stages an annual award ceremony every bit as good as the Oliviers.

WHISKY

Is Scottish. Whiskey is Irish. The Welsh is a large one, boyo.

WHISTLE (to)

Backstage is deemed to bring ill luck. The superstition harks back to days of yore before amplification and electricity. Then, stage directors would remove their teeth and whistle up to the flies. This would suffice for the flymen to know it was time to bring in a cloth or take out a gauze.

A whole series of appropriate different whistles would cover all technical changes, but on a frenetic show, mayhem could ensue if someone started to whistle *Rule Britannia*.

WHITE ENVELOPES

A crisp white daily envelope for your petty cash is always impressive even if it's full of IOUs.

WIEPRZOWINA Z RUSZTU PODAWANA Z SOSEM CZOSNKOWYM

Is, of course, grilled pork served with garlic sauce.

WIG

It goes without saying that wigs play a vital role in modern theatre. However, in this instance I am talking about those worn on stage.

It is a sad fact today that a custom-created wig, woven with the hair of the maidens of Mantua, will set you back as much as a night out with your leading lady, unless it's Monday and the drinks are 3 for 1. This is not only because of the paucity of said maidens; the sheer skills involved are now known to few and so the cost, like season tickets, keep rising ever upwards.

If they and their synthetic rivals from Hair Raisers are beyond your budget, do not despair, here is an affordable alternative:

Take an old hat, in fact any old hat and, using a Stanley knife, cut a crown from its top.

Now stick the crown onto a wig block or an ASM, and dye it (the crown) the colour of the hair required.

Dye is inclined to stain the hands so I prefer to use car spray paint for a nice even finish after brushing on a Dulux undercoat.

Next, nip out and buy a hank of plumber's hemp from the nearest hardware store. This is occasionally Italian so you may be already, in your own way, moving towards that perfect Mantuan model.

If the Stanley knife is still sharp enough, cut the hemp into two equal parts – or if not, use a saw.

This sort of wig should always have a centre parting so smear Copydex, or preferably Superglue, liberally onto the back end of the cap and up and over to the centre and then press down one half of the hemp onto it.

Repeat on the other side, if your fingers are still mobile, and you now have a full cap of hair! Fuss it up a bit and tangle both sets of hemp into each other in a cobweb effect for that really natural look. Spray a really good dose of car paint again, and use lots of lacquer to get those curls to stay.

Finally apply a large dollop of hair oil to give the wig a touch of real lustre. Now you can relax at last and step back to admire your handiwork, but, for God's sake, don't light up a cigarette.

WIG MISTRESS

Better-budgeted productions, if they are musicals or period pieces employ a Wig Mistress. Apart from looking after the cast's wigs, Wig Mistresses are the ladies who make sure your riah is in place before you go out front. Their hot box is useful for heating up your Melton Mowbrays but please note to always treat them gently if they suddenly attack certain wigs with hedge trimmers. The constant effect of inhaling lacquer and acetone can make their mental demeanour rather wobbly after a few years in their trade.

WIND UPS

Are when actors wind up other actors. Wind ups can tick along nicely for a bit but they do tend to run down so don't get involved.

WING IT

When a young choreographer says "Sod it, let's wing it" be sure a first aider is at hand.

The cast will throw themselves into the unfinished routine and the routine will throw the cast into more agony than ecstasy.

WINGS

Nothing to do with Paul McCartney or angels but the sides of the stage hopefully unseen by the audience. Wings are very adaptable. They are used as thoroughfares, quick-change areas and places to store furniture, props and members of the cast when not on stage.

WINGS (Fairy)

Bad news for those of you who still believe in them, but in our line of business fairy wings for productions such as *Peter Pan*, are manufactured from galvanised wire moulded into appropriate frames and covered with taut gauze. That's why so many Tinkerbells wear trusses.

But fairies seldom complain as the glitter and the sequins are worth all the pain.

WISDOM OF SOLOMON (the)

You might think that CSMs would need a bit of this brand of wisdom to deal with all the eternal problems they meet up with on a nightly basis.

If you are a potential CSM your question has to be: "Am I born with it, or do I have to develop it?"

Don't worry. Your question is irrelevant. The one certainty amongst Biblical experts is that the wisdom cannot be attributed to Solomon.

WISE

The acronym for an organisation that I am sure attracts lots of entrance applications – Women in Stage Entertainment.

WIT

As "Brevity is the soul of wit", that's it.

WOLFGANG (the old)

Are said to pad around certain venues on a full moon. Ridiculous, of course, when one's equipped, as I always am, with silver bullets to say nothing of a string of Moldavian garlic for luck.

WOLFGANG (the young)

Refers, of course, to the young Mozart though there are few of us now old enough to personally remember him.

WOMAN

I'm not sure about this year's record holder but the Tallest Woman in the World in 1959 shared the bill at the Empire Sunderland with the Woman with Ten Brains, the World's Fattest Family and the Man who Explodes a Bomb on his Chest. The show was aptly entitled *Would You Believe It*.

WOOD FAMILY (the)

If you hear an actor complaining that the Wood Family are in again, it doesn't mean that some sad clan of stalkers are watching his every move from the front row of the stalls.

He is referring to the empty seats watching his performance. It's an expression that now truly dates him, for few seats these days are made of timber. They're still built to collapse, of course, so if you are in the audience you may end on your arse but you will avoid any splinters.

WORD RUNS

Will sometimes take place on the afternoon of a First Night when the director, having exhausted his vocabulary of encouraging directorial words, suggests that a word run would be fun.

It's the equivalent in enjoyment to Tom Brown's entire class being caned for moral turpitude by Doctor Arnold, but the cast won't take it lying down. They'll rattle through it at breakneck speed, their minds fixed on anything else but the play and so prove once again that a good paraphrase is a good paraphrase and hurts no one save the playwright.

WORKSHOP (a)

Musicals can be long in gestation but many have short lifespans.

One way to lower the odds of this form of infant mortality is to workshop a production.

Once script and score are in some form of playing order, producers often mount workshops to be sure that all the elements of success are there or, at least, to find out potentially if they could be.

Actors are hired specifically for these occasions, the creative team work through the show and, at the end of a week or so, present the whole piece or edited highlights to an invited audience.

These showings are a very important step in the development or death of a production.

Those who come to view the workshop will have a specific interest in the show, be it personal, financial or critical. Their reaction is initially invariably enthusiastic so the producer's next task is to sort out the pleasantries from the truth and determine if his show has a future.

XANADU, YAWN & ZAUBERFLÖTE

X IS FOR:

XANADU

In Xanadu did Kubla Khan
A stately pleasure dome decree:
Where Alph, the sacred river, ran
Through caverns measureless to man
Down to a sunless sea.

I quote these lines from Coleridge so as to answer that second most perennial question concerning *Citizen Kane*. Where did the name of his house come from?

It is also the title of a disastrous film which has, of course, become a cult hit musical.

Coleridge also coined the phrase a "willing suspension of disbelief" in describing an audience's capacity to accept events on stage that they know are unreal. That they do is a sure sign that the show works, which brings us back again to *Xanadu*.

XENOPHOBIA

One phobia that is totally forbidden in our liberal line of work. Anyway, these days, a deep dislike of foreigners will get you into trouble in most parts of the UK.

XERXES (The Great)

Not an early member of the Magic Circle, but the King of Kings of Persia. Few realise that if those six hundred Spartans had not impeded his passage at Thermopylae and Themistocles thrashed his fleet at Salamis, theatre today could be a very different experience for our heritage, as we know it could have been totally destroyed.

The works of Aeschylus, Aristophanes, Sophocles and Euripides could well have been supressed and burnt on the flames of a Zoroastrian temple and, the theatres of Epidaurus, Thoricus and Dionysus reduced to rubble by a Satrap's whim.

X-RATED

X-rated shows are not that common these days, as these days most shows are.

X-RAYS

Should never be beamed into a full auditorium even if it is a *Star Trek* convention.

Xs

Pencil crosses mark the lines or words in a prompt book where standbys or cues are meant to happen.

Whether they do or not is not up to the pencil crosses.

XYLOPHONE (a)

Should never be carried into a pit upside down.

Y IS FOR

YAWNS

Must as a general theatrical rule be smothered at birth. Especially the first born before the beginning of the first read through.

YES

The correct answer to such small questions as "Can we open in a week?"

Remember, producers haven't hired you for your sense of negativity. They want assurances from everybody that their judgement has been correct, that their production of *9/11 – a Two Tower Tragedy* will check in rather than out.

So, as they say, lots of Teeth and Smiles and... Yes, they're putting up the notice.

YES (?)

That tight-lipped question muttered or snarled in the general direction of the corner when an actor realises that he has dried and needs a prompt.

YESTERDAY

In this business starts at curtain down.

YODELLING

Is no longer an indispensible part of an actor's artistic armoury.

Gone is the time when *The Maid of the Mountains* was mounted regularly, these days *The Song of Norway* mostly gets null points and though many White Horse Inns are still undoubtedly open and running, some landlords' musical tastes start with Black Sabbath and end with Iron Maiden. They may put in das cursory boot und hard, should you attempt even one chorus of '*Mein Vater war ein Wandersmann*'.

No, you'll only need this skill today if you find yourself in *The Sound of Music*. But then again, if you're not a Maria, you'll have to be sixteen or under and into goatherds, and that, as well as being rather smelly, can get you into even more trouble.

YORICK

Is merely a skull so if some joker asks if you'll ASM and cover that part tell them you know it not.

YOUNG

You have to be perennially young to join in and join the play.

So, to enjoy yourself at work, may I suggest that you leave age and infirmity at home – even if you do need an ambulance to get you back there.

YOU'RE ON

The terse message that understudies dread, inevitably heard as they're about to relax in the mistaken belief that those they cover are fit and healthy. Most conquer their initial anxiety and arrive to save the show but I knew of one very nervous understudy who refused to wash at home during the run of his engagement. This was in case "You're on" would reach him in the bath and shock cause instant drowning.

Z IS FOR

ZAUBERFLÖTE (Die)

Is, of course, Mozart's much-admired *Magic Flute*.

ZEBRA (a)

A zebra is a four-legged animal with no sense of rhythm.
Zorba (no relation) was Greek and a wonderful two-legged dancer.

ZEITGEIST

A word sometimes deftly used by a director meaning the spirit of the times in his production of the seldom revived *Tinned Teeth for Tito*, part three of that Balkan quartet of plays collectively titled *The Brutal Boulevards*.
It does not refer to the Serbian plum brandy he may be sipping.

ZEPPELIN (a)

The only Musical on record to be set in one is *Bumpy Ride* by Bromley and Osborne.
Duck. It could be flying over this page right now.

ZEPPO

When you're doing your theatre quiz, was the least funny on, but the most successful Marx Brother off, for he became their agent. Not to be confused with –

ZIPPO

Which for all non-smokers is the brand name of an American cigarette lighter and one oft used in stage productions owing to its reliability and rugged good looks.

ZIPS

Keep up a lot of things and others safely tucked away in Theatreland.

ZIZI

Is the quintessential name for a dancer. It was invented in the middle of the last century for the French ballerina Mademoiselle Jeanmaire who in 1949 became an overnight star in London, dancing the role of Carmen in the eponymous ballet choreographed by her husband Roland Petit. Each tortuous step, every diabolically complicated move was, as far as she was concerned just plain 'easy', but, as she was French, it came out as *zizi* and that's how Jeanmaire got her first name.

ZORRO

Has to wear a mask so, if it's your duty to look after this essential piece of costume, please make sure that *both* eyeholes are kept absolutely clean, clear and tidy on a nightly basis.

When you've got him wrapped up in his long flowing cloak, eased into his thigh-length leather boots and all tooled up – a bullwhip in one hand, a rapier in the other and a blazing flambeau clasped between his teeth – it could be that tonight's your lucky show, but remember this may not apply for him, should he become visually impaired for so much as a second.

ZYWIEC

A splendid Polish beer to compliment the grilled pork served with garlic sauce.

You will deserve several of these if you have arrived at this final word of Theatre Lore in one session.

TO BE CONTINUED...

POSTSCRIPT

Some of my more anxious colleagues have pointed out that the definition of 'Petty Cash' is partly missing.

I am afraid I can only reply that I have their legible signatures for any outstanding floats in question.

ACKNOWLEDGEMENTS

My thanks to so many people for their kind interest, especially Dr Mark Bryant for his invaluable help and advice, Duncan Hook for his splendid cover design and computer wizardry and Simon Callow for his generous foreword which, some are bound to say, makes up for the rest of the book.

Finally, a special word of thanks to my very dear friend, the late Simon Bond. Simon's cartoons bring undoubted comic class to the tome and will be very useful for the more illiterate reader.

It was typical of the man that, instead of producing the one cartoon requested, Simon delivered almost the full alphabet. These, I believe, are his last unpublished drawings and so I am very proud to be able to share them with you.

BIOGRAPHIES

THE AUTHOR – NICK BROMLEY

After training at the Central School of Speech and Drama in London, Nick Bromley's theatrical career has been based mainly in the UK, with singular exotic forays to Soweto, Tel Aviv and Salford. He has company and stage-managed more than fifty plays and musicals, including *Love Never Dies* at the Adelphi, *The Sound of Music*, *The King and I* and *Chitty Chitty Bang Bang* at the London Palladium, and, amongst others, the first West End productions of *Starlight Express*, *Crazy For You*, Simon Gray's *Butley*, Alan Ayckbourn's *Absurd Person Singular* and Alan Bennett's *The Old Country*. He has worked as assistant to Orson Welles and is the current Master of the Drury Lane Theatrical Fund. He first met Simon Bond in the late 1970s through a mutual interest in cartoons and together they produced *Sherriffs At The Cinema*, a collection of the celebrated *Punch* artist's film caricatures, which had a tie-in exhibition of the artist's drawings at the National Theatre in London.

THE ARTIST – SIMON BOND

Though he had worked as a stand-up comedian, as a dealer in antiquarian prints and paintings, and as a writer and publisher, Simon Bond (1947-2011) was best known as a cartoonist and illustrator, notably creating the international bestseller, *101 Uses of a Dead Cat* (1981). Born in New York but educated in Britain, he later lived in the USA in the 1970s, contributing to the *Saturday Evening Post*, *Esquire*, *National Lampoon*, *New Yorker* and others. After the success of *101 Uses of a Dead Cat*, which eventually sold more than two million copies and was published in 20 countries, he returned to the UK, working for *Punch*, *Private Eye* and others and producing more books. In all he published more than 20 books, including *Odd Visions and Bizarre Sights* (1983), *Uniformity* (1986), *A Bruise of Bouncers* (1987), *Battered Lawyers and Other Good Ideas* (1989), *Odd Dogs* (1989), *Holy Unacceptable* (1990), *Commuted to Life* (1992), *Everybody's Doing It* (1993) and *101 Uses of a Dead Roach* (2002) with an 'epitaph' by the celebrity drug-dealer Howard 'Mr Nice' Marks. He also wrote and illustrated three children's books featuring his creation the teddy bear Tough Ted. The illustrations he did for *Theatre Lore* were his last published drawings.

SUMMIT FOR HEROES

Any accurate relief map of Theatreland will show how extreme are the contours of its terrain.

Look closely and you may see that the hills are alive with its inhabitants as they climb every mountain to reach that impossible dream.

Avalanches may be encountered, fogs, falls and compulsory oxygen breaks, but somehow most manage to arrive at the top of their particular peak.

The choice of achievement is open. Many are content to stroll up Snowdon, others want to grapple Ben Nevis, some go in hope of mounting the Jungfrau, and a few, a very few, wish to go even higher.

My designer and stage manager Duncan Hook is training to climb Mount Everest for the benefit of Help for Heroes, the charity that provides assistance to all those of our armed forces who have been injured in conflict. Should you wish to support him and donate to this worthy cause, Duncan's website is: http://www.summitforheroes.co.uk.

Thank you.